JL 300

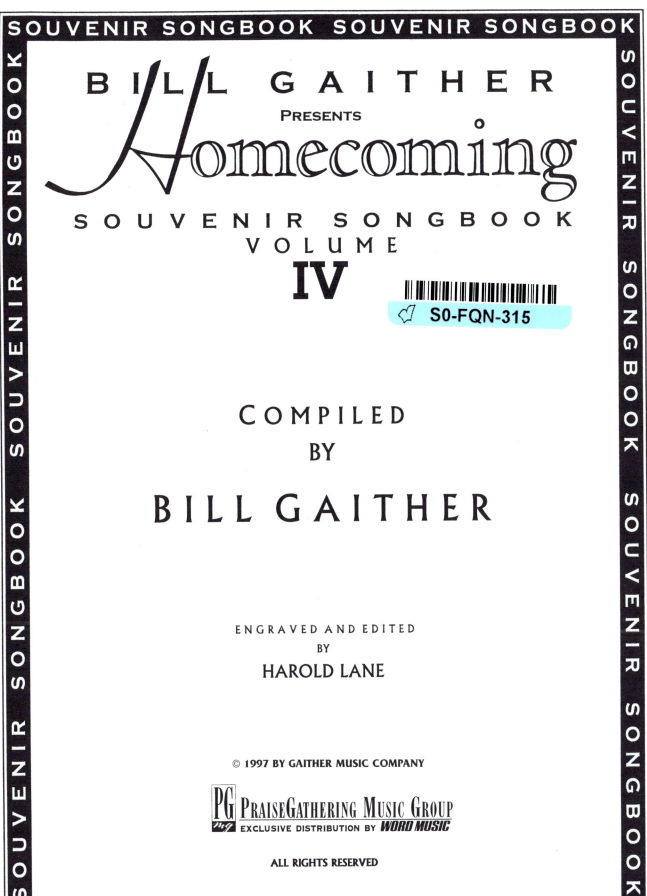

SOUVENIR SONGBOOK SOUVENIR SONGBOOK

BILL GAITHER

Presents

Homecoming

SOUVENIR SONGBOOK
VOLUME
IV

S0-FQN-315

COMPILED
BY

BILL GAITHER

ENGRAVED AND EDITED
BY
HAROLD LANE

PG mg **PraiseGathering Music Group**
EXCLUSIVE DISTRIBUTION BY **WORD MUSIC**

Gaither Music
COMPANY

Foreword

When we started the Homecoming Video Series five years ago, I would not have believed it if someone would have told me that there would be some forty more to follow. And because of all those videos, it required many more songs -- great songs! Many of you have asked for these songs in print. You have also wanted to be there, behind the scenes, to watch what happens. So, we had a photographer capture many of those special moments on camera.

So, here is the fourth souvenir song and picture album which gives you a front-row seat to enjoy and sing along with your friends.

Blessings!

Bill Gaither

And He's Ever Interceding

Carolyn Gillman

Carolyn Gillman

4

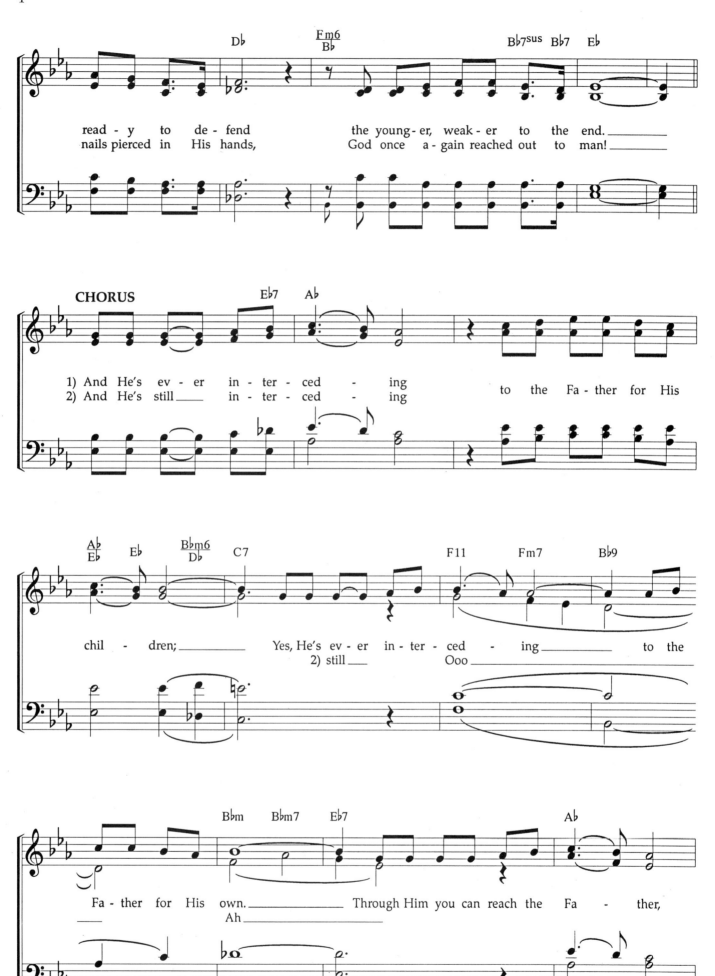

5

So bring Him all your heav-y bur - dens; _____ Yes, for
you He's in-ter-ced - ing, _____ So come bold-ly to the
throne! throne! _____ So come bold-ly to His throne. _____

Tonya Goodman Sykes

Bless His Holy Name

Andraé Crouch   **Andraé Crouch**

Blessed Assurance

Fanny J. Crosby

Phoebe P. Knapp

Daniel Prayed

G. T. Speer

G. T. Speer

1. I heard a - bout a man one day who wast - ed not his
2. They cast him in the li - ons' den be - cause he would not
3. O broth - er, let us watch and pray, like Dan - iel, live from

time a - way, He prayed to God ev - 'ry morn - ing, noon and night;
hon - or men, He prayed to God
day to day,

He cared not for the king's de - cree but trust - ed God to
Their jaws were locked, it made him shout, and God soon brought him
We, too, can glad - ly dare and do the things of God, He'll

set him free, Old Dan - iel prayed ev - 'ry morn - ing, noon and night.
safe - ly out, Old Dan - iel prayed
take us through,

Don't Get Down On Jesus

Joel Hemphill

Joel Hemphill

11

Feeling At Home In The Presence Of Jesus

William J. & Gloria Gaither

William J. Gaither

14

Floodstage

Billy Ready

Billy Ready

THE Gaithers

A Family Portrait

Top row (left to right): Andrew, Benjy, Bill, Barry, Jesse
Bottom row (left to right): Amy, Lee, Gloria, Will, Suzanne

Bill with his mother Lela, father George,
sister Mary Ann and brother Dan

Gloria and grandson, Will

Glen Payne and Guy Penrod singing
"Haven of Rest"

Phil Cross and the Poet Voices

Jerry Clower

Jimmy Blackwood

Terry Blackwood

Jake and the Gatlins

Debra Talley

Cynthia and Ivan

Les Beasley, Jim Hill, Jim Hammil

J.D. doing his ear thing

Buddy Greene

Mrs E.B. (Velda) Hartley -
Bill's former pastor's wife

Kelly Nelon Thompson

The Florida Boys

Squire Parsons

Jessy Dixon

For God So Loved

Jim Hill   **Jim Hill**

1. As the Sav-iour was walk-ing up Cal-v'ry's ___ hill,
2. They put nails in His hands, pierced His pre-cious ___ side,

All the birds stopped their sing-ing, the ___ leaves ___ stood still;
And the pain was so great that tears ___ filled ___ His eyes;

All the flow'rs in the fields bowed their love - ly ___ heads,
Yet, He spoke not a word 'til the last ___ breath He drew,

While the Sav-iour to Cal-v'ry was led. ___
Then He prayed, "They know not what they do." ___

CHORUS

Tell me why, oh, tell me why, did Je-sus die on Cal-va-ry?

Fourth Man

Arthur Smith

Arthur Smith

Here is a sto-ry from the Good Book we know, A sto-ry 'bout a mir-a-cle that hap-pened long a-go; We hope that you'll take cour-age when temp-ta-tions you meet; There's Some-bod-y watch-in' you Who's strong when you're weak. They would-n't bend, They held on-to the will of God, so we are told; they would-n't bow, they would-n't bow their knees to the i-dol made of

CHORUS

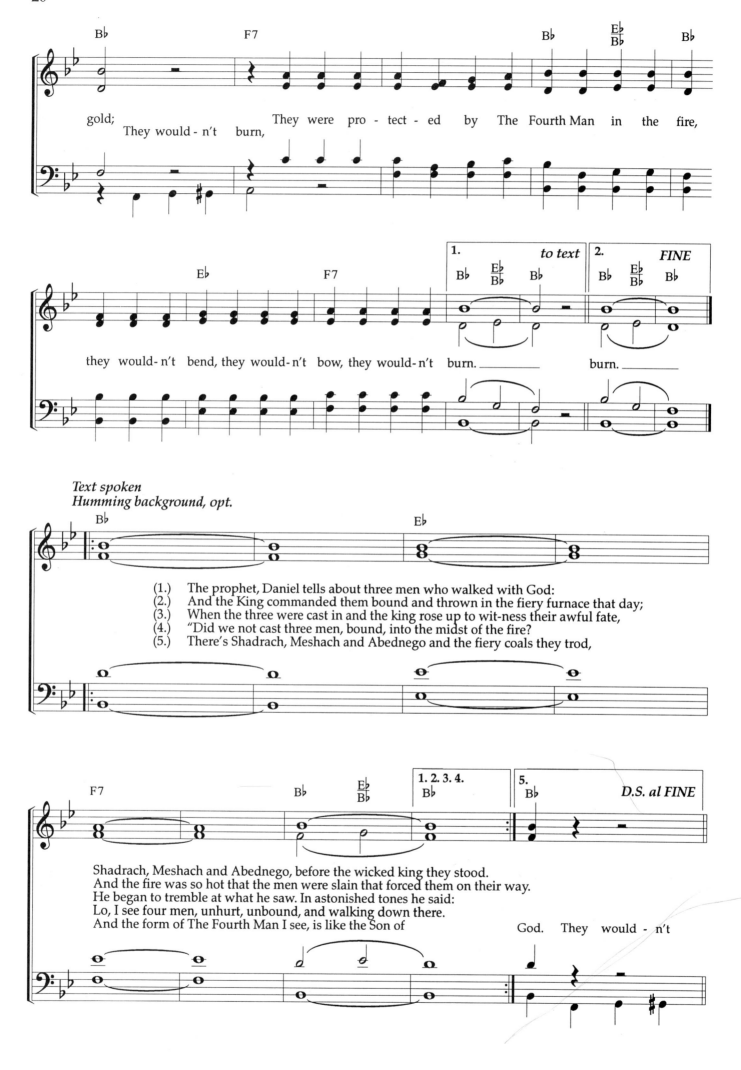

Gettin' Ready Today

Joe Hatfield

Joe Hatfield

1. I wan-na move from this world of fear; Kind-a get-tin' tired___ of liv-in' here; Wan-na go home where the winds___ of___ sor-row nev-er blow;___ Far___ from the shad-ow of the tomb, Far___ from the sad-ness and the gloom; I wan-na go home when death de-mands my tat-tered soul.___ Get-tin' read-y to-day,___

2. I wan-na go home when life is through, Mov-in' out to Heav-en where dreams___ comes true; I can get thrilled just___ think-in' 'bout the glo-ry we___ will share;___ Gon-na see___ loved ones who are gone, Gon-na see the King up-on His throne, And nev-er re-turn to this old life when I___ get there.___

CHORUS

Gettin' Ready To Leave This World

Luther G. Presley

Luther G. Presley

world, Gettin' read-y for the gates
world of sor-row, I'm a-get-tin' read-y for the
world, Gettin' read-y for the gates

sor-row, Read-y, get-tin' read-y for the

of of pearl; Keep-ing watch-ing,
gates of pearl; Keep-ing my re-cord bright, watch-ing,
of pearl; Keep-ing watch-ing, both day and night,

gates of pearl to-mor-row; Keep-ing watch-ing,

Get-tin' read-y to leave this world.
I'm a-get-tin' read-y to leave this sin-ful world.
Get-tin' read-y now to leave this sin-ful world.

Read-y to leave this world.

Joel and LaBreeska Hemphill

Getting Used To The Family Of God

William J. & Gloria Gaither

William J. Gaither

Give Them All To Jesus

Bob Benson, Sr. & Phil Johnson

Bob Benson, Sr. & Phil Johnson

1. Are you tired o' chas-in' _____ pret-ty rain-bows? ____
2. — He nev-er said _____ you'd on-ly see sun-shine, ____

And are you tired o' spin-in' ____
And He ____ nev-er said ____ there'd

— 'round and 'round? _____
be no ____ rain; _____

Wrap up all the shat-
— He on-ly prom-

— ered dreams _____ of your ____ life, ____
— ised a heart full of sing-in', ____

And at the feet of Je-sus lay them down.
A-bout the ver-y things ____ that once brought pain.

CHORUS

Go Ask

Gloria Gaither

William J. Gaither

ask the man____ who's found the way____ through tan - gled roads____ back
ask the child____ who's got a dad____ to love a - way____ the

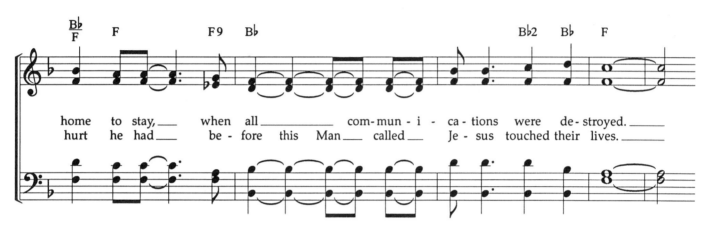

home to stay,____ when all_____ com-mun - i - ca-tions were de-stroyed.____
hurt he had____ be - fore this Man___ called___ Je - sus touched their lives.____

Go ask the child___ who's walk - ing now,___ who once was___ crip-pled___
Go ask the one___ whose fears have fled,___ whose churn - ing heart_____ was

then some-how_____ her use - less legs____ — were made to jump for
qui - et - ed_____ when Some - one____ — whis-pered peace to all her

God On The Mountain

Tracy Dartt

Tracy Dartt

33

God Rides On Wings Of Love

Mike Murdock

Mike Murdock

CHORUS

you're gon-na be free! God rides on the wa- ter. He

rides on the flood.___ There ain't no pow'r from hell gon-na stop God's

wings___ of love. I feel the winds of mer - cy

and the rain from a- bove._____ God_____ rides on

wings___ of love.___ _____ 2. When your back's a-gainst the wall and you

Greater Is He That Is In Me

Lanny Wolfe

Lanny Wolfe

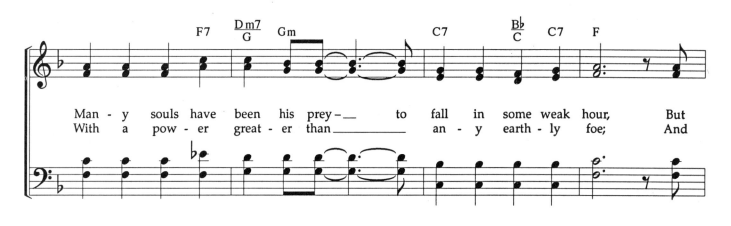

Man - y souls have been his prey—__ to fall in some weak hour, But
With a pow - er great - er than_____ an - y earth - ly foe; And

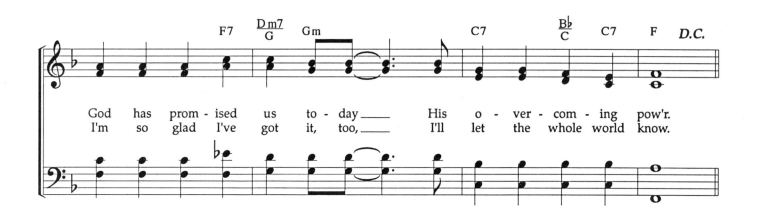

God has prom - ised us to - day____ His o - ver - com - ing pow'r.
I'm so glad I've got it, too,____ I'll let the whole world know.

after 2nd verse

Great - er is He____ that is in me, great - er is He____ that is in me,

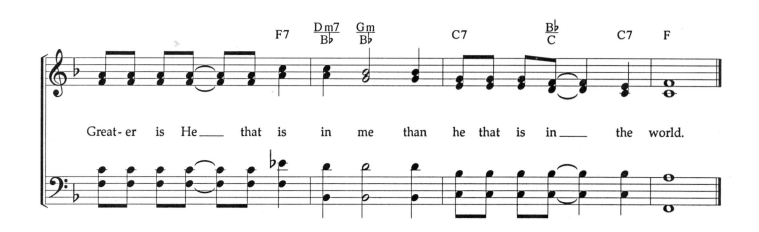

Great - er is He____ that is in me than he that is in____ the world.

Hallelujah Praise The Lamb

Gary McSpadden, Dawn Thomas & Pam Thum **Gary McSpadden, Dawn Thomas & Pam Thum**

40

42

Happiness

William J. Gaither

William J. Gaither

Gospel show has convention center crowd lifting their voices in praise

BY MATTHEW BRADY
FORT WORTH STAR-TELEGRAM

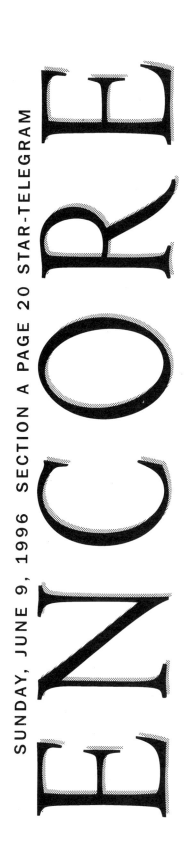

SUNDAY, JUNE 9, 1996 SECTION A PAGE 20 STAR-TELEGRAM

ENCORE

FORT WORTH - More than 14,000 fans packed the Fort Worth/Tarrant County Convention Center last night for a veritable Super Bowl of southern gospel, complete with a Hall of Fame quarterback.

The event, "Homecoming Texas Style," played like cool water to Metroplex music lovers thirsty for four-part harmony. After the evening performance sold out, organizers added a matinee, which promptly sold out as well.

At the 7 p.m. performance, the audience clapped, stomped and sang along to the voices of gospel legends such as Vestal and Howard Goodman, Eva Mae LeFevre, Hovie Lister and Larnelle Harris.

The entire three-hour show played like a highlight film of the past 30 years in gospel music.

Standout performances included Vestal Goodman, who with her husband, Howard, and Johnny Minick, proved that she can still belt out standards like *Clear Title* and *I Wouldn't Take Nothing For My Journey Now*. Also, the family trio, The Martins, sang a simple but piercing a cappella version of the doxology that brought the crowd to its feet.

NFL Hall of Fame quarterback Terry Bradshaw performed a duet with Jake Hess, formerly of The Statesmen, that wasn't half-bad.

Their rendition of *That's Enough* provided a glimpse of what Bradshaw, who lives in Westlake, and Hess hope to offer in an upcoming gospel album, which would be Bradshaw's third.

When they weren't in the spotlight, the performers sat on stage and served as a mass choir. Also backing up the vocalists was a brass and woodwind band, drums and two grand pianos.

Bill Gaither served as master of ceremonies and music director. The event is an outgrowth of a series of videotapes and CD's that Gaither and his wife, Gloria, have produced to chronicle the history of Southern Gospel.

Last night's performance was taped and is scheduled to be broadcast Sept. 7 on The Nashville Network.

Happy Am I

J. M. Henson

J. E. Marsh

1. Sweet-ly I trust in my Re - deem - er as I go sing - ing on my way,
2. Sweet-ly I sing a - long the jour - ney, help - ing the lost to know His love,
3. Look - ing for Him most an - y mo - ment, read - y when Je - sus shall ap - pear,

So hap-py am I, _____ yes, hap-py am I; _____
Yes, so hap-py now, ver - y hap-py now;

Dai - ly I know that He is with me, keep-ing my soul from day to day,
Hop - ing to meet Him in the morn - ing in the e - ter - nal home a - bove,
Keep-ing my lamps all trimmed and burn - ing, feel - ing His com - ing now is near,

So hap-py am I, _____ yes, hap-py am I. _____
hap-py now am I, yes, hap-py am I, yes, hap-py am I.

CHORUS

Happy Rhythm

Mosie Lister Mosie Lister

CHORUS

He Giveth More Grace

Annie Johnson Flint

Hubert Mitchell

1. He giv - eth more grace when the bur - dens grow great - er, He send - eth more
2. When we have ex - haust - ed our store of en - dur - ance, When our strength has

strength when the la - bors in - crease; To add - ed af - flic - tion He
failed ere the day is half done, When we reach the end of our

add - eth His mer - cy, To mul - ti - plied tri - als His mul - ti - plied peace.
hoard - ed re - sourc - es, Our Fa - ther's full giv - ing is on - ly be - gun.

CHORUS

His love has no lim - it, His grace has no meas - ure, His power has no

boundary known unto men; _____ For out of His infinite

rich-es is Je-sus, He giv-eth, and giv-eth, and giv-eth a-gain!

Lily Fern Weatherford

He Knows Just What I Need

Mosie Lister

Mosie Lister

1. My Je-sus knows_____ when I am lone-ly._____ He knows each pain._____
2. My Je-sus knows_____ when I am bur-dened;_____ He knows how much
3. When oth-er friends_____ seem to for-get me, When skies are dark,

He sees each tear._____ He un-der-stands_____ each lone-ly heart-ache;_____
my heart can bear._____ He lifts me up_____ when I am sink-ing,_____
when hope seems gone,_____ By faith I feel_____ His arms a-bout me,_____

He un-der-stands_____ and al-ways cares._____
And brings me joy_____ be-yond com-pare._____
And hear Him say,_____ "You're not a-lone."_____ My Je-sus knows just what I_____

need._____ Oh, yes, He knows just what I_____ need._____ He sat-is-fies_____

and ev-'ry need sup-plies. Yes, He knows just what I_____ need._____

He Pilots My Ship

Ronny Hinson   Ronny Hinson

CHORUS

He Was There All The Time

Gary S. Paxton

Gary S. Paxton

He Will Lead His Children Home

Lonnie B. Combs

Robert R. Christian

He Will Pilot Me

Charles T. Bailey

Byron L. Whitworth

1. Al - though I can - not see the way O'er life's tem - pes - tuous
2. Dark clouds may gath - er in the sky, And rough the sea may
3. Dear Lord, what - e'er the storm may be, I'll sim - ply trust in

sea, dark sea, I know that Je - sus is my Friend, And
be, may be; His love shall ev - er be my song, I
Thee, in Thee, Re - ly - ing on Thy love so true To

that He'll pi - lot me.
know He'll pi - lot me. He'll By pi - His hand He'll
safe - ly lot

CHORUS

pi - lot me, o - ver life's tem - pes - tuous sea,
me from day to day, When

When my blind - ed eyes can't see, can - not see the
blind - ed eyes can't see the

60

He Will Surely Make It All Right

Dee Abernathy & Lee Roy Abernathy

Dee Abernathy & Lee Roy Abernathy

He's A Personal Saviour

Lee Roy Abernathy

Lee Roy Abernathy

1. You've heard ___ a-bout a place called Heav-en up in the blue;
2. Don't ev - er try to quench the Spir-it when God's a-round;

I'm glad ___ that all my sin's for-giv-en, I'm tell-ing you;
Some peo - ple seem to get so near it, then turn Him down;

I'd like ___ to see you get this feel-ing you can re-ceive;
Judg - ment ___ you're gon - na see the Sav-ior that you've passed by.

God's read - y now to give this feel-ing, if you be-lieve.
Think how ___ you're gon - na feel that morn-ing, when oth - ers cry.

CHORUS

Almost time for a break

Lunch time

Food, food

and more food

How sweet it is!

Ivan Parker

Lillie Knauls and Audrey Mieir

Larry Gatlin and Jake Hess take the lead

Ricky and Geraldine...you guess which is which

Jeff and Sheri Easter and brother Rabbit

Rex Nelon

John Starnes

James singing
"I Want to be More Like Jesus"

Two dear friends

Henry Slaughter

Joy Gardner and George Younce

Happy rhythm

Humorist Carl Hurley

Walt Mills and the gang

Mark Lowry

Vestal

Howard Goodman

Hear My Song, Lord

Gloria Gaither

William J. Gaither

CHO. Hear my song, Lord, You fill me with mu - sic,
1. When I am hun - gry — You feed me liv - ing bread.

Hear my words, Lord, You fill me with praise;
When I am thirst - y, — Wa - ter of Life.

Take this mo - ment, I just can't waste it, This one is
I will not fear, You're al - ways with me. Ev - 'ry

Yours, Lord, I give You this day.
need I have, — You sat - is - fy.

His Hand In Mine

Mosie Lister

Mosie Lister

68

Home

Charles Aaron Wilburn & Rusty Goodman
& Tanya Goodman Sykes

Charles Aaron Wilburn & Rusty Goodman
& Tanya Goodman Sykes

1. Home is where___ the heart is, ___ my___ heart's on "home." ___ ___ ___ though I nev-er real-ly had one___ to call my own;___ But I've been giv-en a key,___ by the Car-pen-ter of Gal-i-lee,___ and the in-t'rest paid,___ the

2. Ev-'ry-bod - y dreams___ of go-ing home it seems, ___ late-ly I___ am no ex-cep - tion to the rule;___ But home is so___ much more ___ ___ than win-dows, walls and doors,___ it's a warm em-brace,___ where the

70

CHORUS

Home Where I Belong

Pat Terry

Pat Terry

72

Hotel Hallelu

Randy Phillips

Randy Phillips

75

I Feel Like Traveling On

William Hunter

James D. Vaughan

1. My Heav'n-ly home is bright and fair, I feel like trav-el-ing on;
2. Its glit-t'ring tow'rs the sun out-shines, I feel like trav-el-ing on;
3. Let oth-ers seek a home be-low, I feel like trav-el-ing on;
4. The Lord has been so good to me, I feel like trav-el-ing on;

No pain or death can en-ter there, I feel like trav-el-ing on.
That Heav'n-ly man-sion shall be mine, I feel like trav-el-ing on.
Which flames de-vour, or waves o'er-flow, I feel like trav-el-ing on.
Un-til that bless-ed home I see, I feel like trav-el-ing on.

CHORUS

Yes, I feel like trav-el-ing on,
trav-el-ing on,

I feel like trav-el-ing on;
trav-el-ing on;

My Heav'n-ly home is bright and fair, I feel like trav-el-ing on.

I Go To The Rock

Dottie Rambo

Dottie Rambo

1. Where do I go when there's no one else to turn to?
2. Where do I hide 'til the storms have all passed over?

Who do I talk to when no one wants to lis - ten?
Where do I run to when the winds of sor - row threat - en?

Who do I lean on when there's no foun - da - tion sta - ble?
Is there a ref - uge in the time of trib - u - la - tion?

I go to the Rock I know that's a - ble, I go to the Rock.
— — When my soul needs con - so - la - tion, I go to the Rock.

I Have A Song Inside

Wallace B. Varner

Wallace B. Varner

81

I Have Decided To Follow Jesus

Folk Melody from India

1. I have de - cid - ed_____ to fol - low Je - sus;_____
2. The world be - hind me,_____ the cross be - fore me;_____
3. Tho' none go with me_____ I still will fol - low;_____
4. Will you de - cide now_____ to fol - low Je - sus?_____

I have de - cid - ed_____ to fol - low Je - sus;_____
The world be - hind me,_____ the cross be - fore me;_____
Tho' none go with me_____ I still will fol - low;_____
Will you de - cide now_____ to fol - low Je - sus?_____

I have de - cid - ed_____ to fol - low Je - sus;_____
The world be - hind me,_____ the cross be - fore me;_____
Tho' none go with me_____ I still will fol - low;_____
Will you de - cide now_____ to fol - low Je - sus?_____

No turn - ing back,_____ no turn - ing back._____
No turn - ing back,

I Have Returned

Marijohn Wilkin

Marijohn Wilkin

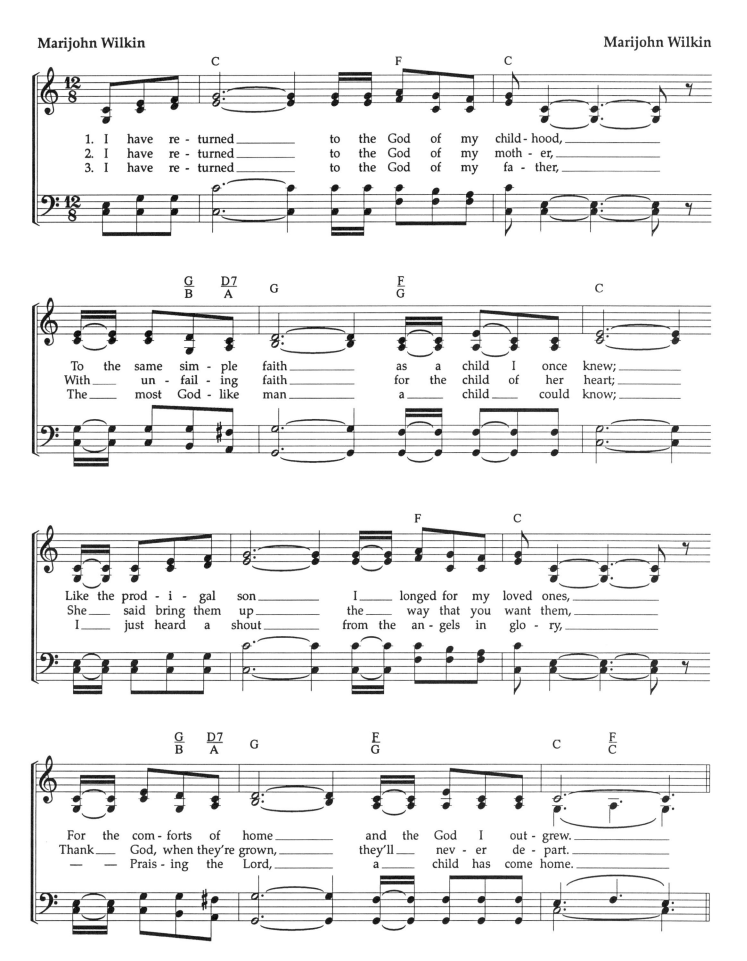

84

CHORUS

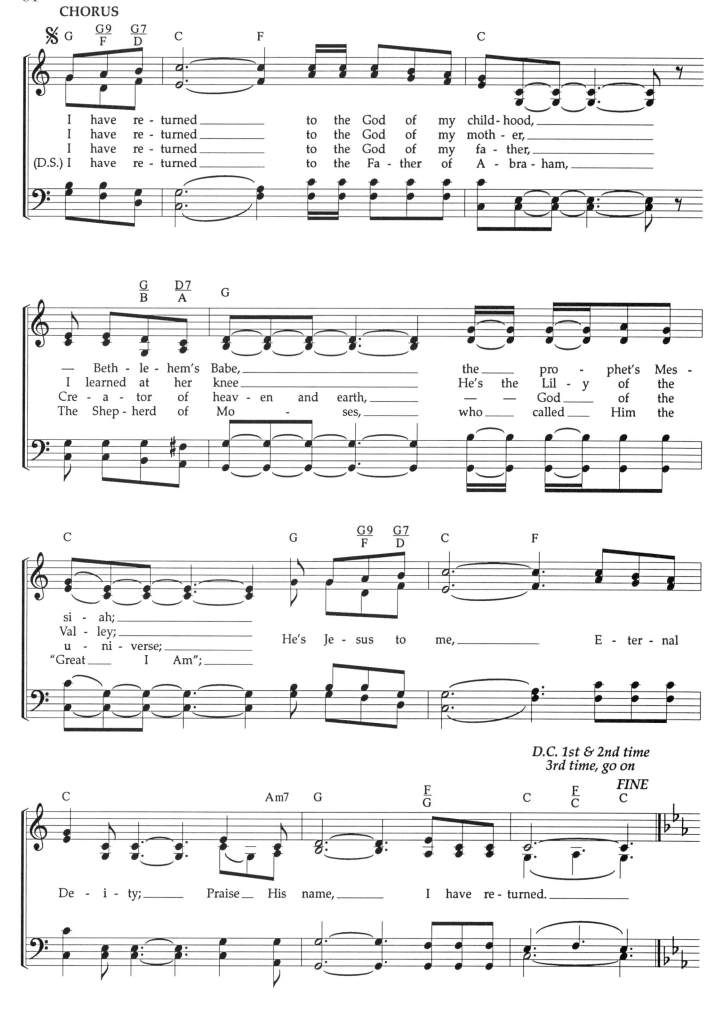

4. I have re - turned_____ to the Yah - weh of Ju - dah,_____

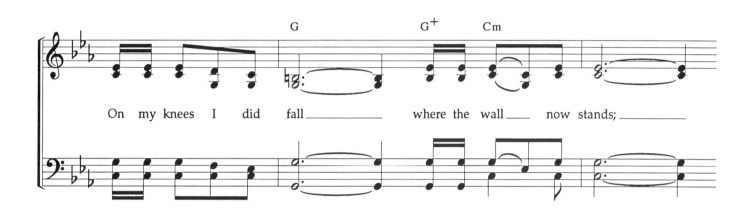

On my knees I did fall_____ where the wall___ now stands;_____

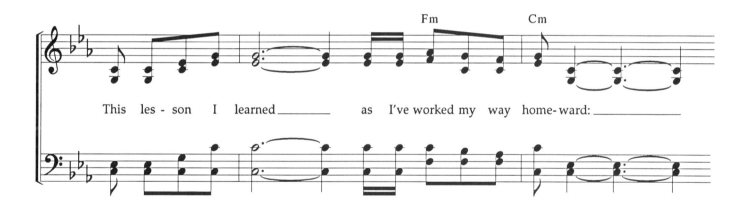

This les - son I learned_____ as I've worked my way home- ward:_____

D.S. al FINE
(To CHORUS)

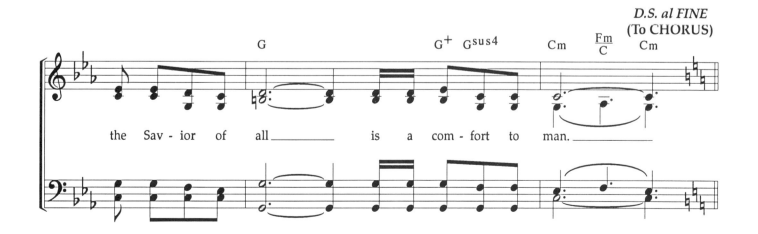

the Sav - ior of all_____ is a com - fort to man._____

I Know

Robert LaVerne Tripp

Robert LaVerne Tripp

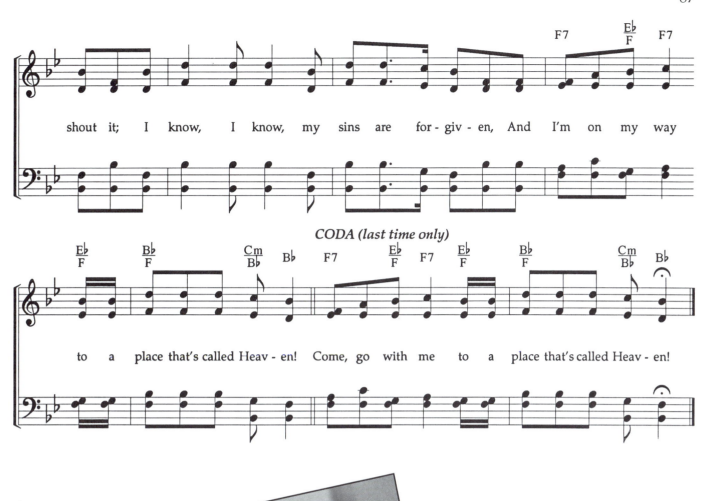

shout it; I know, I know, my sins are for-giv-en, And I'm on my way

CODA (last time only)

to a place that's called Heav-en! Come, go with me to a place that's called Heav-en!

Wesley Prichard

Steve Weatherford

I Need You

Sheri Easter

Sheri Easter

I Shall Wear A Crown

TRADITIONAL

1. Watch - ing, ___ there - fore, ___ you know not ___ the day,

when the ___ Lord shall ___ call your soul ___ a - way;

If you ___ la - bor, ___ striv - in' for the right,

you shall wear a robe ___ and crown. ___

CHORUS

I shall wear a crown. I shall wear a crown, when the

CHORUS 2

94

Bob Cain with Wallace Nelms

I Will Rise Up From My Grave

Jack & Gail Toney

Jack & Gail Toney

I Won't Have To Cross Jordan Alone

Thomas Ramsey & Charles E. Durham

Thomas Ramsey & Charles E. Durham

1. When I come to the river at end - ing of day, when the last winds of sor - row have blown,_____ There'll be Some - bod - y wait - ing to show me the way, I won't have to cross Jor - dan a - lone._____

2. Tho' the bil - lows of sor - row and trou - ble may sweep, Christ, the Sav - ior, will care for His own;_____ 'Til the end of the jour - ney, my soul He will keep, I won't have to cross Jor - dan a - lone._____

CHORUS

I won't have to cross Jor - dan a - lone,_____ Je - sus died all my

Dean Brown

I'll Be True

V. B. (Vep) Ellis

V. B. (Vep) Ellis

I'll Meet You By The River

Albert E. Brumley

Albert E. Brumley

102

I'm Gonna Keep On

William J. Gaither

William J. Gaither

The Happy Goodmans

I'm Saved And I Know That I Am

Ralph H. Goodpasteur

Ralph H. Goodpasteur

I'm Winging My Way Back Home

J. B. Coats

J. B. Coats

I've Been To Calvary

William J. Gaither

William J. Gaither

1. I've nev-er trav-eled far a-round the world,_____ I've nev-er
2. I walked the Cal-v'ry road where Je-sus trod,_____ I saw Him

seen the man-y thrills and sights un-furled;_____ But I have
hang-ing there, the Son of God;_____ With tear-stained

tak-en the jour-ney of jour-neys for me,
eyes I knelt and prayed, "Je-sus, hear_____ my plea,"

Up Cal-v'ry's moun-tain there my Sav-ior to see._____
Oh, praise the Lord, I'm glad I've been to Cal-va-ry._____

110

I've Been With Jesus

Arthur Smith

Arthur Smith

I can feel Him in my soul;
I can feel Him in my soul;

With love He sought me, with blood He
With love He sought me, with blood He bought me,

bought me, I've been with Jesus and I'm whole.
I've been with Je - sus and I'm whole.

Larry Ford and Hovie

I've Never Been This Homesick Before

Dottie Rambo

Dottie Rambo

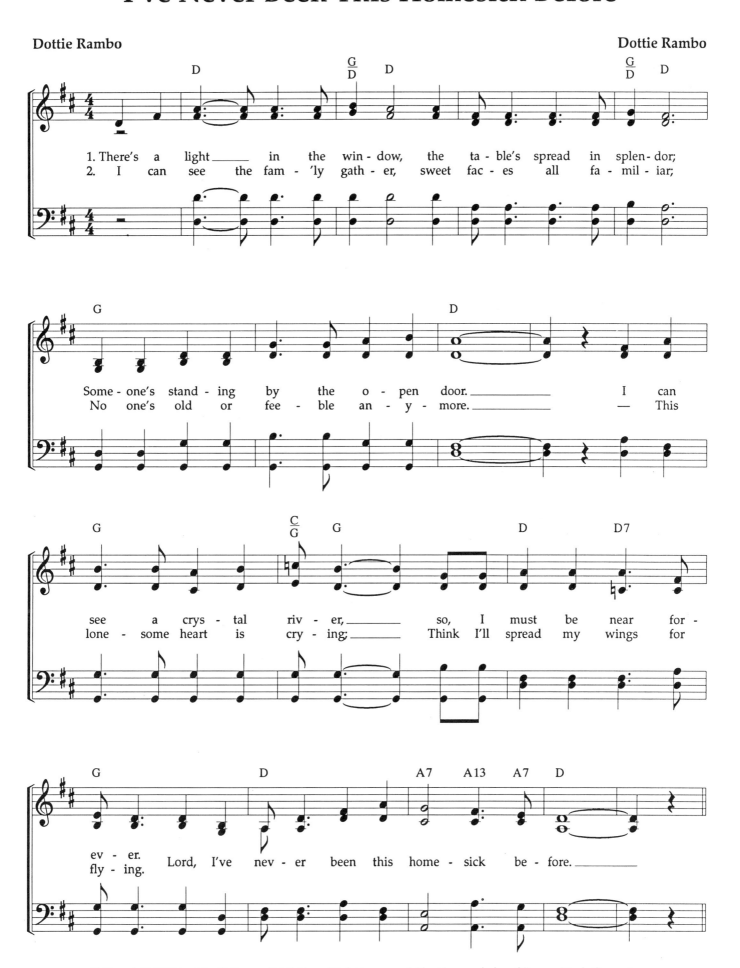

See the bright light shine,_____ It's just a-bout home - time,_____

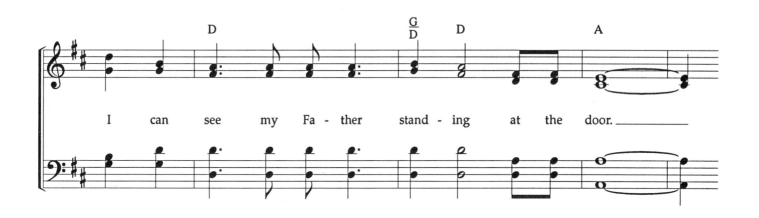

I can see my Fa - ther stand - ing at the door._____

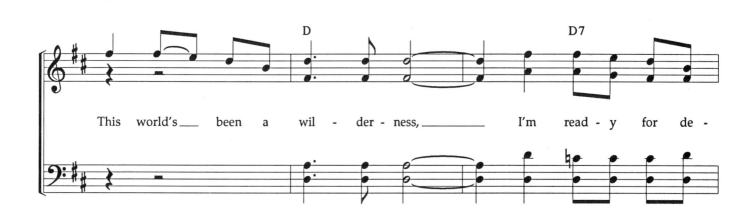

This world's___ been a wil - der - ness,_____ I'm read - y for de -

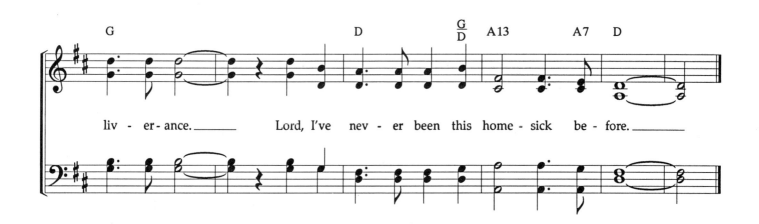

liv - er - ance._____ Lord, I've nev - er been this home - sick be - fore._____

I've Never Seen The Righteous Forsaken

Archie Dennis, Jr.

Archie Dennis, Jr.

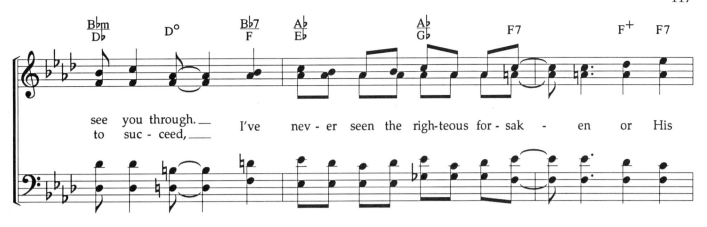

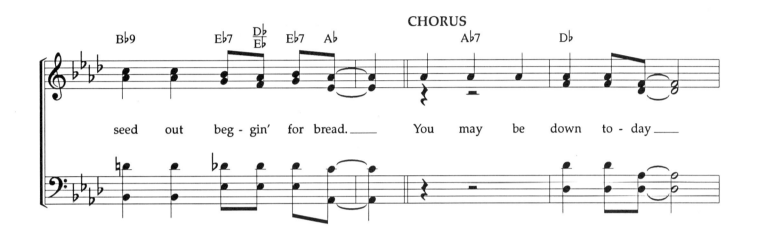

If It Keeps Gettin' Better

William J. Gaither

William J. Gaither

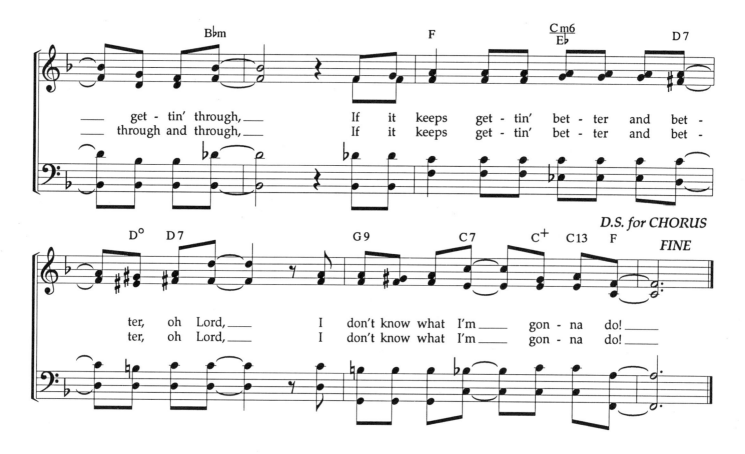

The Original Trio

In The Shelter Of His Arms

Ike Davis & Ray Heady

Ike Davis & Ray Heady

It Is Finished

William J. & Gloria Gaither

William J. Gaither

123

It Will Be Worth It All

William J. Gaither

William J. Gaither

It Won't Rain Always

Gloria Gaither

WIlliam J. Gaither & Aaron Wilburn

126

It's Beginning To Rain

Gloria Gaither & Aaron Wilburn

William J. Gaither & Aaron Wilburn

John the Revelator

Rusty Goodman   **Rusty Goodman**

1. Up - on the Isle of Pat - mos a man was cast one day,
2. While in the Spir - it pray - ing, John turned a - round to see

As he was left a - lone to die,____ he be - gan to pray;
— If the voice____ he had heard was what it seemed to be;

The Ho - ly Ghost fell on him— the Spir - it, It came down,
— Just like man - y wa - ters, a great____ trum - pet sound,

He be - gan to write a - bout the things he saw, The rev - e - la - tor's name was John.
He____ said, "I am____ the First and Last," The rev - e - la - tor wrote it down.

Lift Me Up Above The Shadows

Herbert Buffum & R. E. Winsett

Herbert Buffum & R. E. Winsett

THE TENNESSEAN

June 1996

Old music has a new mission
Gospel great Gaither crusades to preserve tradition

By Robert K. Oermann

You can add a couple of new feathers to the cap of gospel music Hall of Fame member Bill Gaither.

Already renowned for his song writing, showmanship, discovery of young talents and Christian sincerity, Gaither has recently become a TV entrepreneur working to preserve traditional gospel singing. He has been bringing the legends of gospel together for a series of concert specials on The Nashville Network that have been ratings champs. The most recent installment will air at 9 tonight on TNN.

"A lot of early, very important, gospel music history has been lost," says Gaither, "but at least these shows will help. We should have been doing this all along. I

Bill Gaither's greatest fame is as a composer of traditional gospel music, but he also is on a crusade to preserve these tunes.

don't know that I'm a 'savior' of history, but I take a lot of pride in this.

"The country-music field has done very well. I don't care who the hot new act is, they want to sing a song with George Jones or Bill Monroe. I was jealous.

"You show me a man who doesn't know where he's been and I'll show you a man who doesn't know where he is going. It is very important to our children for us to

pass our heritage along to them."

Little has been written about gospel's history. From the mid-1800's onward, revival-meeting songbooks were published that put the religious message in catchier terms than traditional hymns did. Groups toured to popularize the new tunes and eventually became professional entertainers as the recording industry grew in 1920-45. This gave birth to the gospel music field.

After World War II, white gospel quartets adopted pop music showmanship and flashier clothing. Several acts graduated into the pop mainstream, notably the Jordanaires, the Oak Ridge Boys, the Statler Brothers and the Gatlins. At age 60, Gaither is old enough to have witnessed his style's complete rise to modern prominence.

"I was born in 1936. Grew up in a blue-collar home and heard country music from a very early age. But I wasn't particularly attracted to it. It was awfully sad.

"Back in 1948 I turned on the radio and heard a male gospel quartet, a group called the Dixie Four, and just fell in love with the music. I was in the seventh or eighth grade; and I believe that the music that you listen to when you are in junior high becomes the love of your life.

"I loved the harmony, the rhythm, the one-man-band piano player, the low bass. It wasn't necessarily the theology. To be honest with you, I didn't quite know what they were singing. It was just fun. I liked it because it was upbeat."

He formed a gospel quartet as a teen in Alexandria, Ind., but after college he went to work as a school teacher. In his 20's he began to sing locally with a brother and sister. He began writing songs in 1960, married his lyricist wife Gloria in 1963 and became a full-time gospel entertainer in 1968.

Since then the Gaither Vocal Band has been the training ground for many of modern gospel's most prominent singers - Sandy Patti, Larnelle Harris, Michael English, Steve Green, Carman, Don Francisco and current member Mark Lowry. As a result, Bill Gaither is revered throughout his industry as a nurturer of new talent and a bridge to young people.

Gaither's Christian music enterprises included the largest sales outlet for sacred music in the U.S., an aircraft leasing business and a sound/light company used by gospel's superstars.

His annual "Praise Gathering" in Indianapolis, "Family Fest" in Gatlinburg and "Jubilate" in Charlotte have drawn tens of thousands of fans each year. He won Grammy Awards in 1973, 1975 and 1991.

His greatest fame is as a composer. Bill and Gloria Gaither have written more than 400 religious songs, including such standards as *He Touched Me,* *Because He Lives, The King Is Coming* and *There's Something About That Name.*

But his new TV venture may eclipse all his other accomplishments. In 1991 Gaither was recording an album of standards called *Homecoming,* so he invited some of gospel's pioneers to participate and videotaped the proceedings.

"It was really an accident," he recalls.

"We asked a bunch of people who had already retired - Howard and Vestal Goodman, Hovie Lister, J.D. Sumner, Eva Mae LeFevre and people that I've know a long time. The Family Channel and CBN heard about the tape and asked if they could run it. I said, 'Are you serious?' because it was not that good musically and the video was just one camera. But people got so excited and the phone started ringing."

Gaither has since made 20 similar home videos, 11 of which have become TV specials. Now nearly 100 gospel legends participate on stage during the tapings. Last year, Gaither began airing his shows on TNN. The first two were the second most popular programs on the network during the weeks they aired.

These programs not only spotlight the Speers, the Hemphills, James Blackwood, Jake Hess, the Florida Boys, the Nelons, the Cathedrals and other legends, they feature many of gospel's "new breed" entertainers, including Cynthia Clawson, the Martins and current Gaither members Guy Penrod and Jonathan Pierce.

"I don't think we've done great television as an industry," Gaither reflects. "The Statesmen and the Blackwood Brothers were syndicated out of Atlanta; Bob Poole had a national show out of Greenville, S.C., for awhile. Probably the most well known TV show was Gospel Jubilee out of Nashville in the '60s.

"I've found that people are wanting to see this music. I think it's the earthiness. And now young people are asking to come and sing with these old folks. We're taping a new show in Fort Worth on June 8 and we've sold 20,000 tickets."

Gaither has sold more than a million copies of these videos, but says that it's the feeling behind them that counts.

"Gospel really does work. I have genuinely rejoiced. I don't know where I got it, but I hope I will be remembered as a person who genuinely cared about his fellow man." ■

Look On The Brighter Side

E. M. Baygents

Eugene Wright

138

Kirk Talley

Look What The Lord Has Done

Mark David Hanby

Mark David Hanby

142

Lord, Feed Your Children

David Binion

David Binion

Lovest Thou Me

William J. Gaither

William J. Gaither

Midnight Cry

Greg Day & Chuck Day

Greg Day & Chuck Day

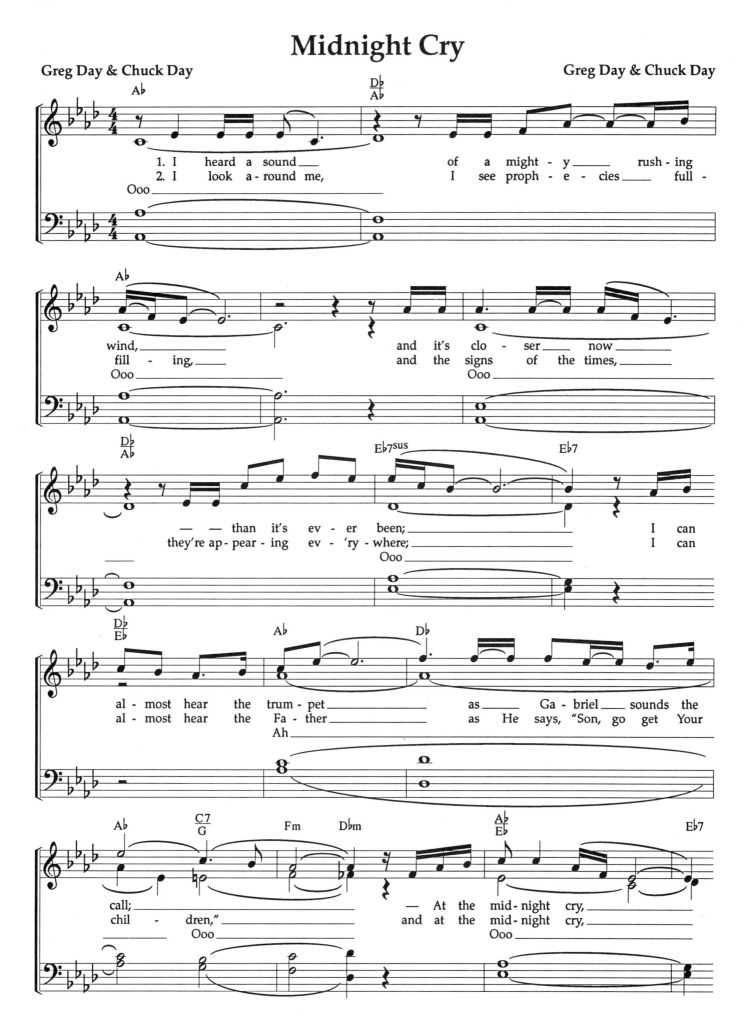

Miracles Will Happen On That Day

Lee Roy Abernathy

Lee Roy Abernathy

More Of You

Gloria Gaither

William J. Gaither & Gary S. Paxton

CHORUS

No One Cared So Much

Jim Hill

Jim Hill

154

No Tears In Heaven

Robert S. Arnold

Robert S. Arnold

Nothing's Too Big For My God

Nancy Harmon

Nancy Harmon

Now I Have Everything

Charles Vandell & David Ingles

Charles Vandell & David Ingles

1. I had noth-ing____ but heart-aches and trou-ble,____ I was seek-ing____ for____ for-tune and fame;____ I had noth-ing____ but doubts and____ con-fu-sion,____ but now I have ev-'ry-thing.____
2. I was mak-ing____ big plans for my fu-ture,____ I was liv-ing____ my____ life-time in vain;____ Then I prayed____ for life's on-ly mean-ing,____ and now I have ev-'ry-thing.____

CHO. gave me life e-ter-nal,____ and now I have ev-'ry-thing.____

CHORUS

Ev-'ry-thing I____ need to make me hap-py,____ I have Je-sus____ to show me the way.____ He has saved me and He

O For A Thousand Tongues

Arranger and producer Lari Goss

The Martins

Lisa Daggs

The Kingsmen Quartet

The McDuff Brothers

Karen Peck and Roger Bennett

Karen Wheaton

David Ring

"When one shares a heartache,
we all share the tears"

"The Glory Came Down"

Sue Dodge

J.D. and The Stamps

Scott Fowler

Mark Speer, son of Brock and Faye

Larry Gatlin, The Singing Weatherfords, George,
Glen and Henry Slaughter at the piano

Joy!

Ronnie Goss

George who?

The Isaacs

Howard gettin' down!

Three great basses

Oh, How Much He Cares For Me

162

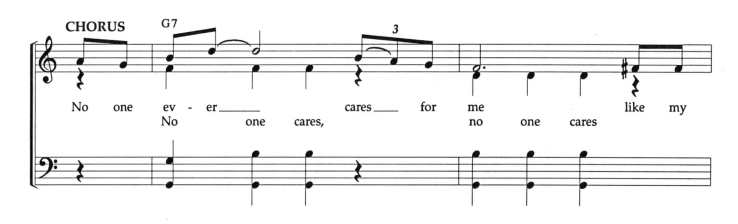

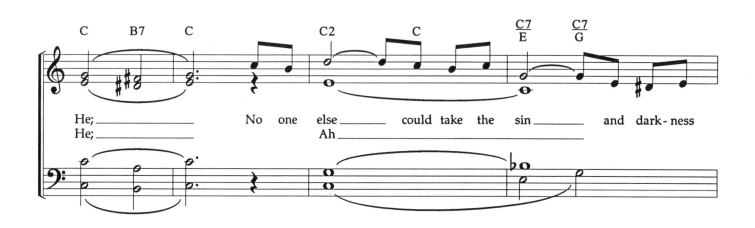

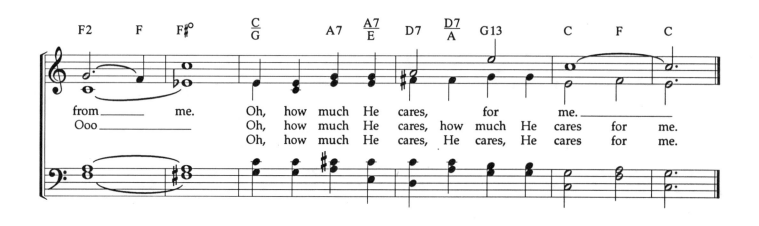

On The Sunny Banks

Dottie Rambo

Dottie Rambo

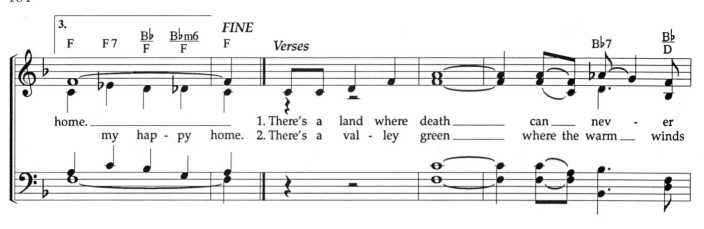

home.
my hap-py home. 1. There's a land where death____ can__ nev- er
2. There's a val-ley green____ where the warm__ winds

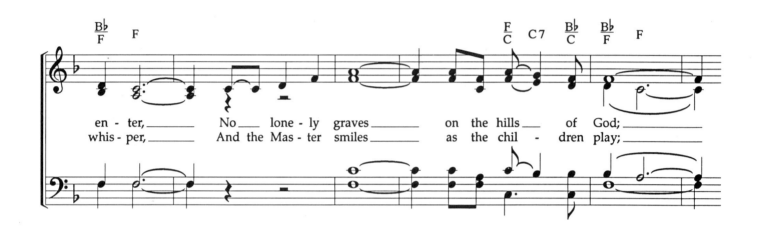

en-ter,____ No__ lone-ly graves____ on the hills__ of God;____
whis-per,____ And the Mas-ter smiles____ as the chil - dren play;____

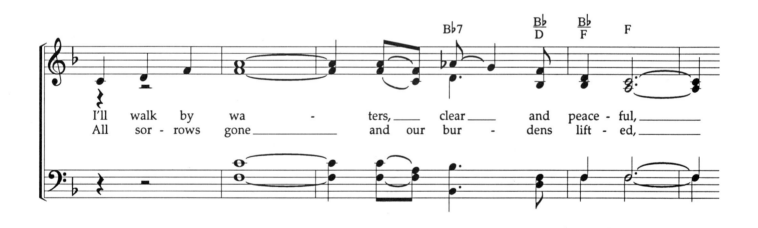

I'll walk by wa - ters,____ clear____ and peace-ful,____
All sor-rows gone____ and our bur - dens lift-ed,____

Where wick - ed men____ shall__ nev - er trod.____
For God Him - self____ wipes the tears__ a - way.____

Out Of His Great Love

Terri & Barbi Franklin

Terri & Barbi Franklin

Over The Moon

V. B. (Vep) Ellis

V. B. (Vep) Ellis

Sing Your Blues Away

Wallace B. Varner

Wallace B. Varner

170

Speak To The Mountain

Marcia Henry

Marcia Henry

1. From strength to strength we some-times go;____ then a - gain we're sink-ing low,
2. In ____ the midst ____ of the bat - tle when the foe is gain-ing ground,

In the shad - ow ____ of a moun - tain loom - ing high a - bove our
— Look up ____ and see the might - y hand of God ____ reach - ing

heads; We need not fear what lies a - head ____ for the Word has clear - ly
down; — Speak God's name; — Sa - tan trem - bles. Speak God's Word and watch him

said, That our faith would be suf - fi - cient to make the moun - tain dis - ap - pear.
flee. Once a - gain our God de - liv - ers, the moun-tain crum - bles at our feet.

CHORUS

Speak to the moun-tain; you'll not tri-umph o-ver me. Be thou re-

moved from here to yon-der,_____ dis-ap-pear in-to the sea. Speak

to the moun-tain; speak with au-thor-i-ty,_____ And the

moun-tain must move and you shall claim vic-to-ry._____

Sunday Meetin' Time

Mosie Lister

Mosie Lister

Thank God For The Promise Of Spring

William J. & Gloria Gaither

William J. Gaither

1. Though the skies be gray a-bove me, And I can't see the light of day; There's a ray break-ing through the shad-ows, And His smile can't be far a-way. Thank God

2. Though the earth seems bleak and bar-ren, And the seeds lay brown and dead; Oh, the prom-ise of life throbs with-in them, And I know spring is just a-head.

FINE CHORUS

D.S. God for the prom-ise of spring.

Thank God for the prom-ise of Spring-time, Once a-gain my heart will sing; There's a brand new day a-dawn-ing, Thank

D.S. al FINE

Thank God I Am Free

James McFall

James McFall

That Old Time Preacher Man

Albert E. Brumley

Albert E. Brumley

1. Well, I went down to the big camp meet-in', 'Twas most for to see___ the sight,
2. He led three songs for the con-gre-ga-tion, and knelt in a word___ of pray'r,

But I got such a heart-y greet-in' that I went back ev-'ry night;
He turned to chap-ter five in Mat-thew and he took his text from there;

They had an old-time gos-pel preach-er, From the good Book he sol-emn-ly read,
He preached the real old-time sal-va-tion, and he cer-tain-ly proved___ him-self,

But when he start-ed preach-in' 'bout soul sal-va-tion, you ought-a heard the things___ he said.
For af-ter he ex-tend-ed the in-vi-ta-tion there was-n't man-y sin-ners left.

CHORUS

You ought-a heard_____ him, when he preached the bless-ed ho-ly Word.

179

That's Enough

Traditional

The Altar

Ray Boltz & Steve Millikan

Ray Boltz & Steve Millikan

1. The ser - vice is near - ing an end, The
2. A fa - ther is pray - ing with his son, The A

choir is sing - ing "Just As I Am." And
moth - er kneels be - side them, thank - ing God they've come. An

now as the old song is played, peo - ple at the al - tar
old man is stand - ing there in tears, giv - ing up a part of him

are kneel - ing down to pray, And some are find - ing mer - cy,
that he's held back for years. Hearts are be - ing bro - ken,

186

The Haven Of Rest

H. L. Gilmour

George D. Moore

1. My soul, in sad ex - ile, was out on life's sea, So bur - dened with
2. I yield - ed my - self to His ten - der em - brace, And, faith tak - ing
3. The song of my soul, since the Lord made me whole, Has been the old

sin and dis - tressed; ___ 'Til I heard a sweet voice say - ing, "Make Me your choice,"
hold of the Word; ___ My ___ fet - ters fell off, and I an - chored my soul,
sto - ry so blest ___ Of ___ Je - sus, who'll save who - so - ev - er will have

And I en - tered the Ha - ven of Rest. ___
The ___ Ha - ven of Rest is my Lord. ___ I've an - chored my soul in the
A ___ home in the Ha - ven of Rest. ___

Ha - ven of Rest, I'll ___ sail the wide seas ___ no more; ___ The tem - pest may

sweep o'er the wild, storm - y deep, In Je - sus I'm safe ev - er - more. ___

The Lord Still Lives In This Old House

Bill R. Burns

Bill R. Burns

CHORUS

The Love Of Jesus

Charles Johnson   Charles Johnson

CHORUS

The Night Before Easter

Don Sumner & Dwayne Friend

Don Sumner & Dwayne Friend

193

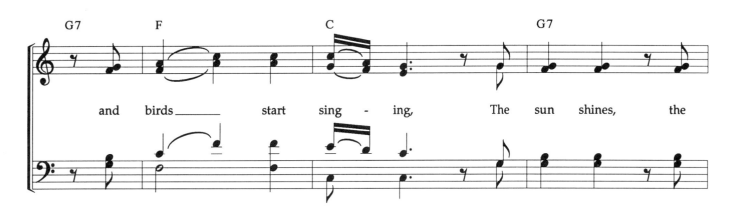

and birds_____ start sing - ing, The sun shines, the

earth warms, for new life it's bring - ing, A lit - tle boy stops

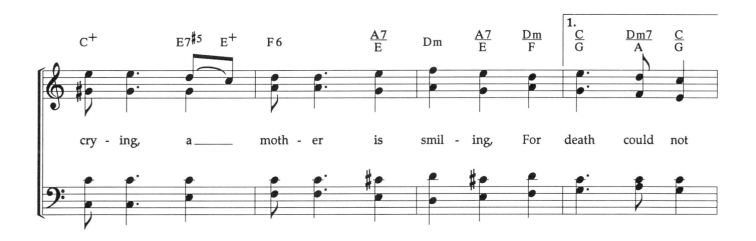

cry - ing, a____ moth - er is smil - ing, For death could not

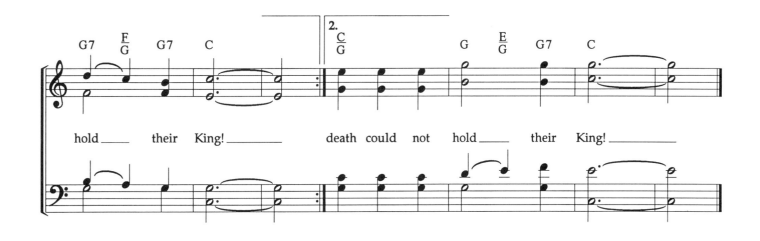

hold____ their King!_____ death could not hold____ their King!_____

The Ninety And Nine

Elizabeth C. Clephane

Ira D. Sankey

1. There were nine - ty and nine that safe - ly lay in the shel - ter ___ of the
2. "Lord, ___ Thou ___ hast here Thy nine - ty and nine; are ___ they not e - nough for
3. But ___ none of the ran - somed ev - er knew how ___ deep were the wa - ters
4. "Lord, ___ whence are those blood - drops all ___ the way that ___ mark out the moun - tain's
5. But ___ all through the moun - tains, thun - der - riv'n, and ___ up from the rock - y

fold, But ___ one ___ was out on the hills a - way, far ___ off from the
Thee?" But the Shep - herd made an - swer: "This of Mine has ___ wan - dered a -
crossed, Nor how dark was the night that the Lord passed through ere He found His ___
track?" "They were shed ___ for one who had gone a - stray ere the Shep - herd could
steep, There a - rose a glad cry to the gate of Heav'n, "Re - joice! I have

gates ___ of gold A - way on the moun - tains wild and bare, a -
way ___ from Me, And al - though ___ the road ___ be rough and steep, I
sheep that was lost. — — Out in the des - ert He heard its cry —
bring ___ him back." "Lord, ___ whence are Thy hands ___ so rent and torn?" "They're
found ___ my sheep!" And the an - gels ech - oed a - round the throne, "Re -

way from the ten - der Shep - herd's care, a - way from the ten - der Shep - herd's care.
go to the des - ert to find ___ My sheep, I go to the des - ert to find ___ My sheep."
sick ___ and help - less and read - y to die, — sick ___ and help - less and read - y to die.
pierced ___ to - night ___ by man - y a thorn, they're pierced ___ to - night ___ by man - y a thorn."
joice, for the Lord ___ brings back ___ His own! Re - joice for the Lord ___ brings back ___ His own!"

The Old Fashioned Meeting

Herbert Buffum

Herbert Buffum

1. Oh, how well I re-mem-ber in the old-fash-ioned days,
2. There was sing-ing, such sing-ing of those old-fash-ioned airs!
3. Well, they say it is bet-ter, "Things have changed, don't you know,"
4. If the Lord nev-er chang-es, as the fash-ions of men,

When the old-fash-ioned peo-ple had some old-fash-ioned ways;
There was pow-er, such pow-er in those old-fash-ioned prayers,
And the peo-ple such in gen-'ral seem to think it is so;
If He's al-ways the same, why, He is old-fash-ioned, then!

In the old-fash-ioned meet-ings as they tar-ried there,
An old-fash-ioned con-vic-tion made the sin-ner pray,
And they call me old-fash-ioned when I dare to say,
As an old-fash-ioned sin-ner saved through old-time grace,

In the old-fash-ioned man-ner, how God an-swered their prayer.
And the Lord heard and saved him in the old-fash-ioned way.
That I like it far bet-ter in the old-fash-ioned way.
Oh, I'm sure He will take me to an old-fash-ioned place.

The Prettiest Flowers Will Be Blooming

Albert E. Brumley

Albert E. Brumley

1. I know there is a land of beau-ti-ful flow-ers, Where we will meet a-gain when life is o'er; Where we will while a-way the end-less hours On Heav-en's bright e-ter-nal shore.

2. On Heav-en's gold-en strand there'll be no more dy-ing, No chill-ing winds or tem-pest e'er will blow; It is a land of love and won-drous beau-ty Where frag-rant flow-ers ev-er grow.

3. I want to meet you by that beau-ti-ful riv-er On that e-ter-nal morn-ing in the sky; Where we will live in peace through end-less a-ges, Where we will nev-er say "good-by."

CHORUS

The pret-ti-est beds of flow-ers will be bloom-ing Pret-ti-est beds of flow-ers there will bloom,

198

Ann Downing

Humorist Dennis Swanberg

The Statue Of Liberty

Neil Enloe

Neil Enloe

Good to have Jim Murry back

The Wicked Shall Cease Their Troubling

203

The World Didn't Give It To Me

Gloria Gaither & Gary S. Paxton

William J. Gaither & Gary S. Paxton

206

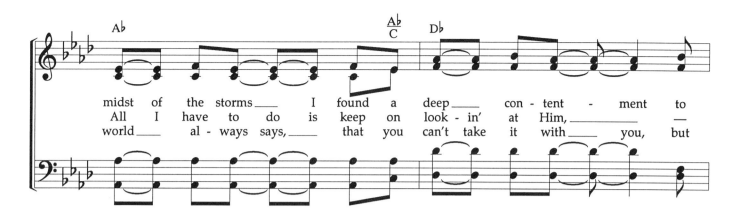

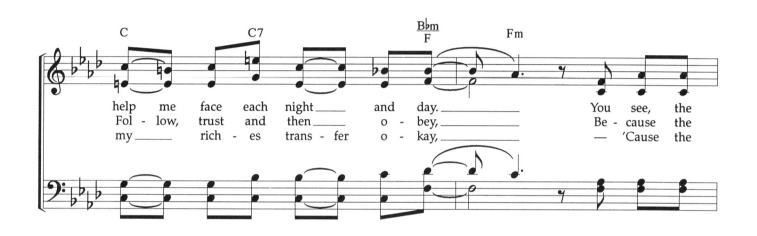

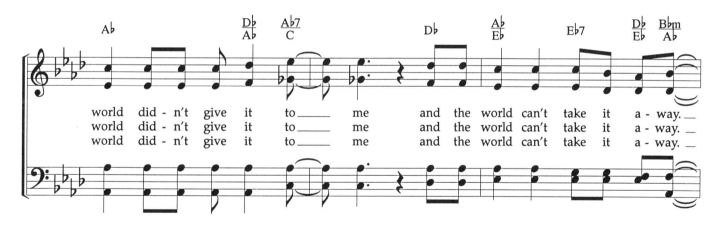

D.C. to CHORUS ⊕ *CODA*

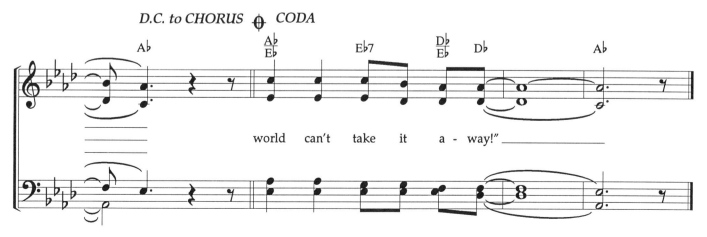

There Is A River

David Sapp

David Sapp

This Great Caravan Keeps On Rolling Along

V. B. (Vep) Ellis

V. B. (Vep) Ellis

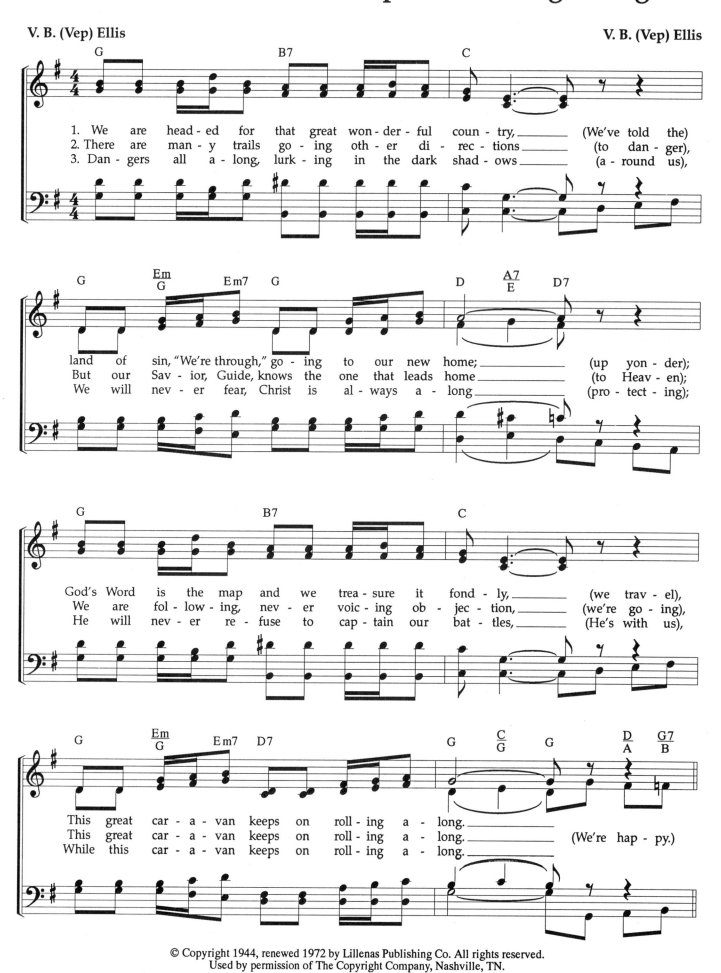

1. We are head-ed for that great won-der-ful coun-try, _____ (We've told the)
2. There are man-y trails go-ing oth-er di-rec-tions _____ (to dan-ger),
3. Dan-gers all a-long, lurk-ing in the dark shad-ows _____ (a-round us),

land of sin, "We're through," go-ing to our new home; _____ (up yon-der);
But our Sav-ior, Guide, knows the one that leads home _____ (to Heav-en);
We will nev-er fear, Christ is al-ways a-long _____ (pro-tect-ing);

God's Word is the map and we trea-sure it fond-ly, _____ (we trav-el),
We are fol-low-ing, nev-er voic-ing ob-jec-tion, _____ (we're go-ing),
He will nev-er re-fuse to cap-tain our bat-tles, _____ (He's with us),

This great car-a-van keeps on roll-ing a-long. _____
This great car-a-van keeps on roll-ing a-long. _____ (We're hap-py.)
While this car-a-van keeps on roll-ing a-long. _____

To Me, It's So Wonderful To Know
Jesus Is Mine

Ralph H. Goodpasteur

Ralph H. Goodpasteur

Trust And Obey

James H. Sammis

Daniel B. Towner

1. When we walk with the Lord in the light of His Word, What a glo - ry He
2. Not a shad - ow can rise, not a cloud in the skies, But His smile quick - ly
3. Not a bur - den we bear, not a sor - row we share, But our toil He doth
4. Then in fel - low - ship sweet we will sit at His feet, Or we'll walk by His

sheds on our way!___ While we do His good will, He a - bides with us still,
drives it a - way;___ Not a doubt or a fear, Not a sigh or a tear
rich - ly re - pay;___ Not a grief or a loss, Not a frown or a cross,
side in the way;___ What He says we will do, Where He sends we will go,

and with all who will trust and o - bey.
can re - main when we trust and o - bey.
But is blest if we trust and o - bey.
Nev - er fear, on - ly trust and o - bey.
Trust and o - bey, for there's

no oth - er way To be hap - py in Je - sus, but to trust and o - bey.

Wait'll You See My Brand New Home

Rusty Goodman

Rusty Goodman

1. If you're awed by this world and all its beau-ty, Man-y state-ly
2. My new home will not be set up-on foun-da-tions, That are made by

man-sions dai-ly you may see, But with-out great wealth I
man and will some-day pass a-way, It won't be built where the

know I'll nev-er own one, and you will nei-ther, if you're
storms of life can bat-ter, where the storm-clouds of-ten

no more rich than me; But if your soul will look be-
hide the light of day; But the Cor-ner-stone of

yond what man is build-ing, you can see what earth-ly
God is my foun-da-tion, the Root of Da-vid, Christ, the

216

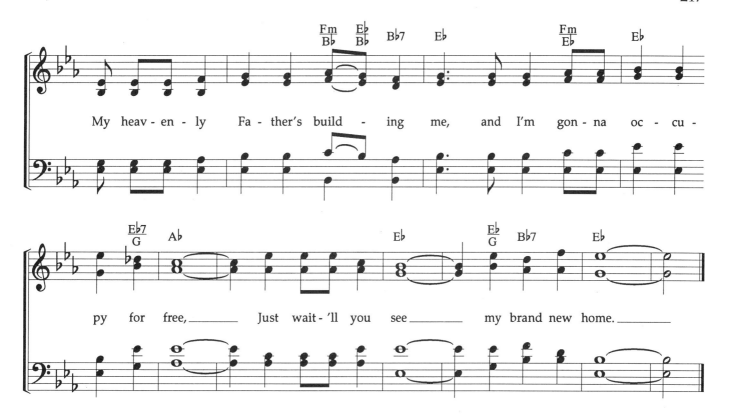

My heav-en-ly Fa-ther's build-ing me, and I'm gon-na oc-cu-

py for free,_____ Just wait-'ll you see_____ my brand new home._____

Jimmy Jones

What A Lovely Name

Charles B. Wycuff

Charles B. Wycuff

1. There's a name a-bove all oth-ers, _____ Won-der-ful to hear, _____ bring-ing hope and cheer; _____ It's the love-ly name of Je - sus, _____ ev-er-more the same, _____ what a love-ly name! _____
2. Through His name there's won-drous pow-er, _____ Pow-er to re-deem, _____ mak-ing sin-ners clean; _____ By His pow'r He cleansed the lep-er, _____ o - pened blind-ed eyes, _____ cause the dead to rise.
3. He'll re-turn in clouds of glo-ry, _____ Saints of ev-'ry race _____ shall be-hold His face; _____ With Him en-ter Heav-en's cit - y, _____ ev-er to ac-claim, _____ "What a love-ly name!" _____

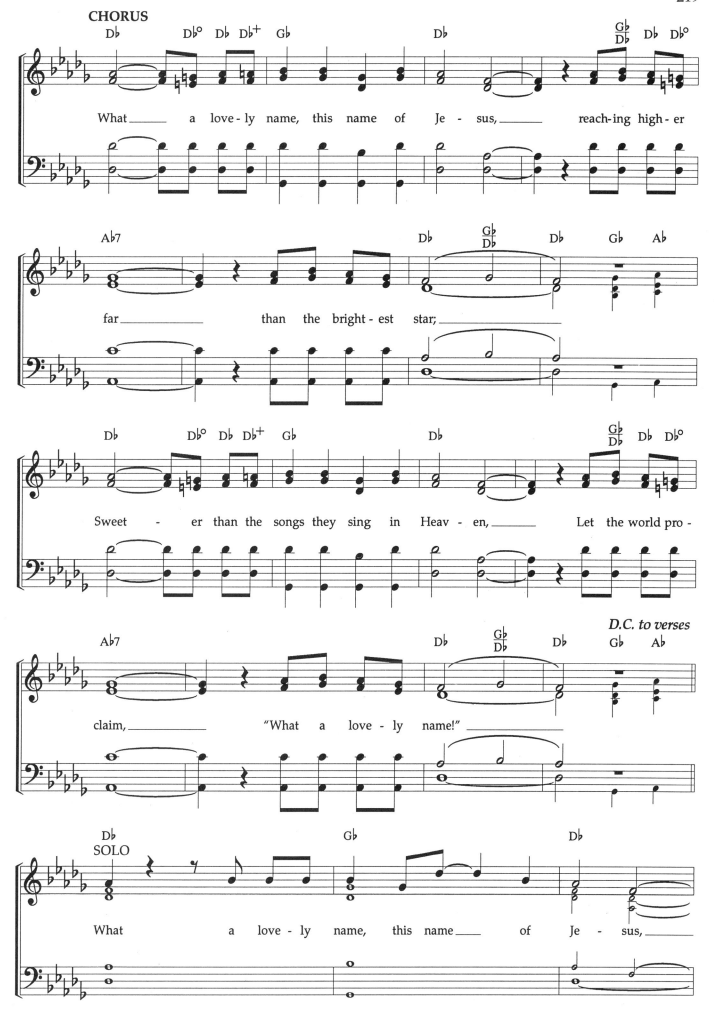

220

When He Blessed My Soul

J. R. Baxter & Cleavant Derricks

J. R. Baxter & Cleavant Derricks

1. Je - sus washed my sin a - way one glo - ri - ous morn - ing, _____ praise His dear name,
2. Je - sus made my spir - it glad
3. Je - sus claimed me as His own

He blessed my soul _____ and He made me whole; _____
He blessed my soul He made me whole;

Ev - er since that hap - py day I'm tell - ing the sto - ry, _____ praise His dear name,
Ev - er to the lone and sad
Ev - er since this joy I've known

How He washed my sin a - way when He blessed my soul. _____
when He blessed my soul.

222

When I Got Saved

V. B. (Vep) Ellis

V. B. (Vep) Ellis

1. Wan-d'ring from God and right,___ my soul was lost (down-heart-ed),
2. I can't af-ford to stop,___ Heav-en is mine (e-ter-nal),
3. If Heav-en you would win,___ tell sin, "good-by" (for-ev-er),

Trav-'ling in dark-est night___ by tem-pest tossed (and driv-en);
I'll sure-ly reach the top___ some hap-py time (up yon-der);
Let Je-sus Christ come in___ be-fore you die (in dark-ness);

Then Je-sus saw my plight___ by sin de-praved (con-vict-ed),
Heav-en is now my goal,___ I can't de-lay (don't stop me),
Up-on Mount Cal-va-ry___ His life He gave (a ran-som),

He came and found me, light shone a-round me, when I got saved.
Soon I'll be leav-ing, I won't be griev-ing, I'm on my way.
His pow'r will fill you, com-fort and thrill you, your soul will save.

CHORUS

I got hap-py down___ in my heart,
Oh, glo-ry, I got hap-py down in my heart,

224

When Jesus Says It's Enough

Joel Hemphill & LaBreeska Hemphill

Joel Hemphill & LaBreeska Hemphill

1. The dis - ci - ples met a storm___ on the boat that night,___ "We're___ go - ing down,"___ they cried.___ But they had for - got - ten that Je - sus said,___ "We're go - ing to the oth - er side." The Mas - ter a - rose and spoke___ to the wind___ and they saw the storm___ o - bey. Je - sus said,___ "It's e - nough," and it went___ a - way.___

CHORUS

When Je-sus speaks peace to my sit-u-a-tion, all my sor-rows

have to flee.____ I know He is a-ware____ and____ He

real-ly cares a-bout all____ that per-tains to me.____ I've had my share____

of trou-ble and tri-als, some-times the go-ing gets rough;____

But when Je-sus says,____ "It's e-nough," it-'ll be e-nough.____

When They Ring The Bells Of Heaven

Albert E. Brumley & Marion W. Easterling

Albert E. Brumley & Marion W. Easterling

1. That will be a hap-py morn-ing o - ver the sea,
2. Ev - er - last - ing glo - ry and an un - end - ing song,
3. Press a - long, re - joic - ing, through this un - friend - ly land,

When the cares of life shall pass a - way; (shall pass a - way for - ev - er;)
With our great Re - deem - er we shall stay; (with Him we'll stay for - ev - er;)
Glo - ry - land is wait - ing o'er the way; (the sun is al - ways shin - ing;)

Mu - sic there to wel - come all the ran - somed and free,
We shall join our loved ones in that Heav - en - ly throng, When they shall
That will be a glad home - com - ing, won't it be grand?

Ring the bells of Heav - en on that day.
day. O hal - le - lu - jah! When they

Yes, I Know!

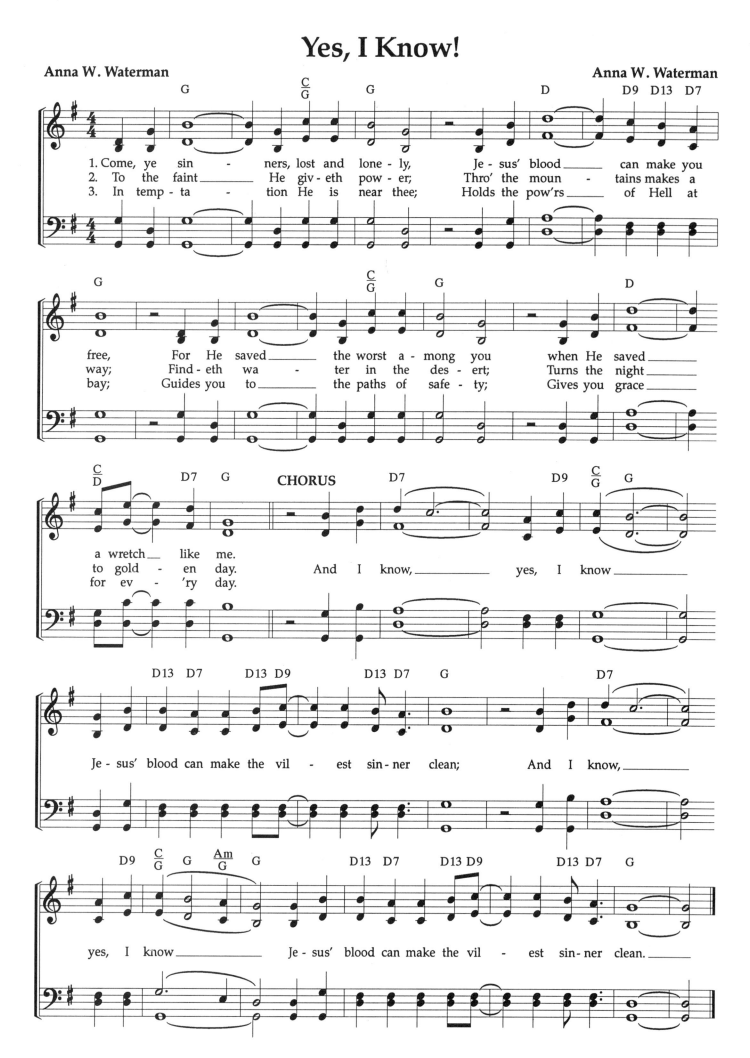

You And Me Jesus

Artists Appearing In Gaither Video Series

-A-

Jacob Aranza
850 Kaliste Saloom, Suite 210
Lafayette, LA 70508
318-237-2264

Assurance
Brian Free
P.O. Box 1909
Douglasville, GA 30135
Mgr., Harper and Assoc.
615-851-4500

-B-

The Bishops (Kenny)
P.O. Box 211
Waco, KY 40385
606-369-3635

Larry Black
P.O. Box 210483
Nashville, TN 37221
615-646-8059

Billy Blackwood
102 Dillon Drive
Hendersonville, TN 37075
615-824-9077

James Blackwood
4411 E. Sequoia
Memphis, TN 38117
901-683-5711

Jimmy Blackwood
P.O. Box 280932
Memphis, TN 38168
800-476-7749

R. W. Blackwood
Rt. 4 Box 3084
Galena, MO 65656
417-272-3927

Terry Blackwood
P.O. Box 40921
Nashville, TN 37204
615-386-9552

Ray Boltz
Ray Boltz Music, Inc.
4205 Hillsboro Rd., Suite 209
Nashville, TN 37215
615-460-0066

Jean Bradford
Rt 3 Box 31
Trenton, GA 30752
706-398-2090

Dean & Mary Brown
P.O. Box 580
Cordova, TN 38088
941-455-3737

Anthony Burger
P.O. Box 680877
Franklin, TN 37068-0877
615-591-3366

Don Butler
P.O. Box 3584
Brentwood, TN 37204

-C-

Bob Cain
3532 Stonehenge Place
Birmingham, AL 35210
205-956-9492

Candy Hemphill Christmas
326 Draper Circle
Goodlettsville, TN 37072
615-859-5010

Jack Clark
P.O. Box 5555
Cleveland, TN 37320
423-479-1200

Cynthia Clawson
Servant's Quarters
P.O. Box 840625
Houston, TX 77284
713-345-7735

Jerry Clower
P.O. Box 121089
Nashville, TN 37212
c/o Tandy Rice/Top Billing
615-327-1133

Elmer Cole
P.O. Box 331
Lookout Mountain, TN 37350
706-820-2356
    or 615-843-1118

Jim Cole
1305 McChesney Avenue
Nashville, TN 37216
Mgr., John Taylor
615-377-3131

Dr. H. Frank Collins
4001 88th Place
Lubbock, TX 79423
806-798-2723

Conrad Cook
  & The Calvary Echoes
Box 186
McConnell, WV 25633
423-688-9808

The Couriers
507 Harrisburg Pike
Dillsburg, PA 17019-1338
(717) 432-8266

Bob Crews
The Harmoneers
6354 Cornelia Drive
Douglasville, GA 30134
770-949-2657

Phil Cross
   and The Poet Voices
Century II
P.O. Box 40707
Nashville, TN 37204
615-385-5700

-D-

Lisa Daggs
Manager, Homeland Records
274 Mallory Station Road
Franklin, TN 37067
615-771-0811 #100

Geron Davis
P.O. Box 8169
Alexandria, LA 71303
318-448-9300

Ken Davis
6080 W 82nd Drive
Arvada, CO 80003
303-425-1319

The Dixie Melody Boys
513 Harding Avenue
Kinston, NC 28501
919-523-9306

Jessy Dixon
P.O. Box 336
Crete, IL 60417
708-672-8682

Sue Dodge
c/o Capital Church
7903 Westpark Drive
McLean, VA 22102
703-760-8888

Ann Downing
Downing Ministries
P.O. Box 767
Hendersonville, TN 37077
615-822-1900

-E-

Jeff & Sheri Easter
2429 Washington Highway
Lincolnton, GA 30817
Mgr., Century II
615-385-5700

Michael English
P.O. Box 681598
Franklin, TN 37068-1589

-F-

Barbara Fairchild
P.O. Box 1693
Branson, MO 65615
417-334-6400

Fairfield Four
Lee Olsen, Manager
c/o Keith Case & Associates
59 Music Square West
Nashville, TN 37203
615-327-4646

The Florida Boys
Les Beasley, Manager
910 East Kingsfield Road
Cantonment, FL 32533
904-968-6052

Larry Ford
2670 Jackson Street
Fort Myers, FL 33901-5064
941-332-4429

Amy Susan Foster
P.O. Box 111802
Nashville, TN 37222
615-331-7285

Eldridge Fox
The Kingsmen Quartet
P.O. Box 2622
Asheville, NC 28802
704-254-5046

Terry and Barbi Franklin
P.O. Box 17164
Nashville, TN 37217-0164
615-360-6104

Deacon Freeman
P.O. Box 311
Rocky Face, GA 30740
706-278-5835

-G-

Danny Gaither
403 Park Avenue
Alexandria, IN 46001
317-724-3039

Joy Gardner
c/o Christ Church
15354 Old Hickory Blvd.
Nashville, TN 37211
615-834-6171

The Gatlins
Larry, Rudy, Steve
c/o Gatlin Bros. Theater
2901 Fantasy Way
Myrtle Beach, SC 29577

The Happy Goodmans
Rick Goodman, Manager
P.O. Box 158778
Nashville, TN 37215
615-370-0777

Mrs. Rusty Goodman (Billie)
P.O. Box 834
LaVergne, TN 37086
615-320-0988

Greater Vision
P.O. Box 158766
Nashville, TN 37215
Mgr., Fay Shedd
615-383-9136

Buddy Greene
P.O. Box 3687
Brentwood, TN 37024
615-377-1251

Hilton Griswold
P.O. Box 202
Plainfield, IL 60544
815-723-6596

-H-
John Hall
P.O. Box 820344
Ft. Worth, TX 76182
817-498-8725

Suzy Hamblen
P.O. Box 1937
Canyon Country, CA 91386

Nancy Harmon
P.O. Box 210369
Bedford, TX 76095
817-498-5683

The Hayes Family
5111 Bamboo Road
Boone, NC 28607
704-264-3806

Heaven Bound
Jeff Gibson
P.O. Box 40707
Nashville, TN 37204
Mgr., Century II
615-385-5700

Joel and LaBreeska Hemphill
3551 Dickerson Rd.
Nashville, TN 37207
615-865-7282

Jake Hess
7827 Kolven Cove
Columbus, GA 31909
706-569-5461

Lou Wills Hildreth
P.O. Box 271106
Houston, TX 77277
713-662-2908

Jim Hill
5916 Valleybrook Road
Middletown, OH 45044
Church 513-422-1021

Wayne Hilliard
P.O. Box 121173
Nashville, TN 37212-0829
615-370-8352

Robbie Hiner
R.R. 3, Box 236
Lynchburg, VA 24504
804-832-2003

The New Hinsons
Ronny Hinson
Century II Promotion
P.O. Box 40707
Nashville, TN 37204-0707
615-385-5700

The Hoppers
Claude and Connie
2811 US #220
Madison, NC 27025
910-548-2968

Carl Hurley
c/o Mike McKinney
P.O. Box 5162
Louisville, KY 40205
502-583-8222

-I-
The Isaacs
131 McNelley Drive
LaFollette, TN 37766
423-566-8527

-J-
Judy Jacobs
P.O. Box 891
Cleveland, TN 37364-0891
423-559-0173

Gordon Jensen
P.O. Box 100512
Nashville, TN 37210
615-451-0090

Bob & Jeanne Johnson
3227 Wiseman Drive
Charlotte, NC 28227
704-531-0701

Charles Johnson
  & The Revivers
Canaan Records
1011 16th Ave. South
Nashville, TN 37212
615-327-1240

LaDonna Gatlin Johnson
P.O. Box 488
Lindale, TX 75771
903-882-4191

Jane Greene Johnson
Marty Johnson
521 Scenic Drive
Morristown, TN 37813
423-581-7959

Phil Johnson
c/o Spring Hill Music
2021 Richard Jones Road
Nashville, TN 37215
615-383-5535

Jimmy Jones
429 Riverview Road
Mableton, GA 30059
404-696-3910

-K-

The Kingsmen Quartet
P.O. Box 2622
Asheville, NC 28802
704-254-5046

Lillie Knauls
P.O. Box 608062
Orlando, FL 32860
407-298-4782

-L-

Harold Lane
2028 Franklin Limestone Ct.
Nashville, TN 37217
615-361-8606

Amy Lambert
P.O. Box 3601
Boone, NC 28607
704-264-8299

Wally & Ginger Laxson
R.R. 3, Box 122
Athens, AL 35611
205-232-7563

Eva Mae LeFevre
4545 River Parkway 7-F
Atlanta, GA 30339
770-952-5330

Mylon LeFevre
P.O. Box 822148
Ft. Worth, TX 76182-2148
817-281-2700

Hovie Lister
  and the Statesmen
P.O. Box 15501
Atlanta, GA 30333
404-371-8992

Mosie Lister
c/o Lillenas Publishing Co.
P.O. Box 419527
Kansas City, MO 64141

Mark Lowry
P.O. Box 967
Brentwood, TN 37024
Mgr., Duane Ward
615-771-7017

-M-

Jack Marshall
P.O. Box 40250
Tuscaloosa, AL 35404
205-553-8621

The Martins
410 Ashley 271 Road
Hamburg, AR 71646
501-853-5819

Babbie Mason
1480-F Terrell Mill Road,
Suite 291
Marietta, GA 30067
770-952-1443

The McDuffs
P.O. Box 190
Pasadena, TX 77501
800-495-7928

Gene McDonald
2025 Bradley, Apt. #2
Kennett, MO 63857
573-888-1034

The McKameys
c/o Ruben Bean
P.O. Box 128
Clinton, TN 37716
423-457-3678

Gary McSpadden
First Choice Tours
P.O. Box 50
Nashville, TN 37202
615-254-5550

Chuck Millhuff
Millhuff Ministries
P.O. Box 160
Olathe, KS 66051
913-764-0000

Walt Mills
P.O. Box 1428
Arlington, TX 76004-1428
817-265-2739

Buddy Mullins
P.O. Box 445
LaVergne, TN 37086
615-793-7335

The Mullins
c/o Roger Mullins
P.O. Box 629
Stockbridge, GA 30281
615-385-5700

Danny Murray
Lee College
1120 N. Ocoee
Cleveland, TN 37311
423-614-8320

Jim Murray
P.O. Box 1521
Hendersonville, TN 37077-1521
615-451-2655

-N-

Rex Nelon/The Nelons
P.O. Box 460
Smyrna, GA 30081
770-434-8181

Calvin Newton
P.O. Box 375
Lookout Mountain, TN 37350
706-398-2822

-O-

Doug Oldham
1600 Belfield Place
Lynchburg, VA 24503
804-384-6951

-P-

Palmetto State Quartet
Jack Pittman
P.O. Box 1507
Greenville, SC 29602
803-246-3599

Ivan Parker
P.O. Box 346
Mount Juliet, TN 37122
615-758-4060

Squire Parsons
P.O. Box 279
Leicester, NC 28748
704-683-1145

Janet Paschal
Janet Paschal Ministries
1719 West End Ave. Ste. 610W
Nashville, TN 37203
Bus. Mgr., Tony Stogsdill
615-329-9007

Roy Pauley
1935 S. Conway Road, B-1
Orlando, FL 32812
407-382-6325

Glen Payne
The Cathedrals
P.O. Box 1512
Stow, OH 44224
Mgr., Eddie Harper
615-851-4500

Karen Peck & New River
RR 4, Box 532, Yahoola Road
Dahlonega, GA 30533
706-864-2082

Guy Penrod
P.O. Box 681744
Franklin, TN 37068

The Pfeifers
711 Washington Ave.
Washington Court House, OH
  43160
614-335-9641

Chonda Pierce
Michael Smith & Assoc.
1024 17th Ave., S.
Nashville, TN 37212
Contact: Mike Smith
615-327-1372

Jonathan H. Pierce
P.O. Box 1207
Franklin, TN 37605
Contact: Scott Greene
615-790-8300

Rosa Nell (Speer) Powell
The Speer Family
54 Music Square West
Nashville, TN 37203
615-327-2728

Wesley Pritchard
4107 Bent Grass Drive
Fayetteville, NC 28301
910-323-5313

-R-

Geraldine Ragan
2203 Inverness Lane
Birmingham, AL 35242
205-980-5971

Dottie Rambo
Rambo Evangelistic Assoc.
P.O. Box 50478
Nashville, TN 37205
615-826-0809

Lynda Randle
4130 NW 79th Street, Apt. 11
Kansas City, MO 64151
816-353-6131

David Reece
612 Fedders Drive
Madison, TN 37115

Mary Tom (Speer) Reid
Ben Speer Music
54 Music Square West
Nashville, TN 37203
615-329-9999

David Ring
c/o Danny DeArmas
P.O. Box 1986
Orlando, FL 32803
407-648-5432

Mrs. Rosie (Betty) Rozell
P.O. Box 706
Trussville, AL 35173
205-856-2874

-S-

The Scotts
Century II Promotions
523 Heather Place
Nashville, TN 37204-3113
615-385-5700

Naomi and the Segos
Naomi Sego (Reader)
P.O. Box 269
Centerville, GA 31028
912-953-5261

Jeff Silvey
2245 Quarry Road
Mount Juliet, TN 37122-3117
615-320-5951

Henry & Hazel Slaughter
P.O. Box 70073
Nashville, TN 37207
615-746-2307

Allison Speer
c/o Brian Speer
54 Music Square West
Nashville, TN 37203
615-329-3535

Ben Speer
Ben Speer Music
54 Music Square West
Nashville, TN 37203
615-329-9999

Brock & Faye Speer
The Speer Family
54 Music Square West
Nashville, TN 37203
615-327-2728

Kevin Spencer Family
2327 Holtz Road
Shelby, OH 44875
419-347-8474

The Stamps
J. D. Sumner
P.O. Box 150532
Nashville, TN 37215
615-383-2887

John Starnes
P.O. Box 3529
Brentwood, TN 37024
615-371-8797

Gordon Stoker
The Jordanaires
P.O. Box 159014
Nashville, TN 37215
615-661-4332

Donnie Sumner
P.O. Box 104505
Nashville, TN 37214
615-885-5681

Dennis Swanberg
Program Resources
P.O. Box 22307
Louisville, KY 40252
502-339-1653

Tanya Goodman Sykes
107 Lake Forest Drive
LaVergne, TN 37086
615-320-0988

-T-

Kirk Talley
P.O. Box 6568
Knoxville, TN 37914
423-522-8800

Roger & Debra Talley
P.O. Box 1918
Morristown, TN 37816-1918
423-235-2916

Kelly Nelon Thompson
P.O. Box 460
Smyrna, GA 30081
770-434-8181

Joe Thrasher
825 Brentwood Pointe, II
Brentwood, TN 37027
615-371-4279

Tiffany-Marie
c/o Noran Spurr
P.O. Box 521776
Longwood, FL 32750
407-830-6636

Alden Toney
3318 Player Drive
New Port Richey, FL 34655
813-376-7626

Jack Toney
209 Sparks Avenue
Boaz, AL 35957
205-593-5454

-V-

Wally Varner
1493 Avenue I S.W.
Winter Haven, FL 33880
941-293-9516

-W-

Hovie Walker
P.O. Box 60143
Nashville, TN 37206
615-226-0244

The Weatherfords
Lily Weatherford
P.O. Box 116
Paoli, OK 73074-0116
405-484-7212

Karen Wheaton
P.O. Box 5137
Decatur, AL 35601-5501
Mgr., Gina Smith
800-345-2736

Aaron Wilburn
123 Susan Drive
Hendersonville, TN 37075
615-326-2733

Daryl Williams
P.O. Box 833
Antioch, TN 37011
615-731-4740

Kevin Williams
P.O. Box 120632
Nashville, TN 37212
615-386-0445

Bob Wills
P.O. Box 8006
Ft. Worth, TX 76124
817-535-0136

Calvin Wills
P.O. Box 211
Arlington, TX 76004
817-572-1414

Willie Wynn
18123 N.W. 60 Ct.
Miami, FL 33015
305-825-9880

-Y-

George Younce
The Cathedrals
P.O. Box 1512
Stow, OH 44224
Manager: Eddie Harper
615-851-4500

TABLE OF CONTENTS

3. AND HE'S EVER INTERCEDING
6. BLESS HIS HOLY NAME
7. BLESSED ASSURANCE
8. DANIEL PRAYED
10. DON'T GET DOWN ON JESUS
12. FEELING AT HOME IN THE PRESENCE OF JESUS
15. FLOODSTAGE
17. FOR GOD SO LOVED
19. FOURTH MAN
21. GETTIN' READY TODAY
23. GETTIN' READY TO LEAVE THIS WORLD
25. GETTING USED TO THE FAMILY OF GOD
27. GIVE THEM ALL TO JESUS
29. GO ASK
32. GOD ON THE MOUNTAIN
34. GOD RIDES ON WINGS OF LOVE
37. GREATER IS HE THAT IS IN ME
39. HALLELUJAH PRAISE THE LAMB
43. HAPPINESS
46. HAPPY AM I
48. HAPPY RHYTHM
50. HE GIVETH MORE GRACE
52. HE KNOWS JUST WHAT I NEED
53. HE PILOTS MY SHIP
55. HE WAS THERE ALL THE TIME
56. HE WILL LEAD HIS CHILDREN HOME
58. HE WILL PILOT ME
60. HE WILL SURELY MAKE IT ALL RIGHT
62. HE'S A PERSONAL SAVIOUR
65. HEAR MY SONG, LORD
67. HIS HAND IN MINE
69. HOME
71. HOME WHERE I BELONG
73. HOTEL HALLELU
76. I FEEL LIKE TRAVELING ON
77. I GO TO THE ROCK
79. I HAVE A SONG INSIDE
82. I HAVE DECIDED TO FOLLOW JESUS
83. I HAVE RETURNED
86. I KNOW
88. I NEED YOU
90. I SHALL WEAR A CROWN
95. I WILL RISE UP FROM MY GRAVE
97. I WON'T HAVE TO CROSS JORDAN ALONE
99. I'LL BE TRUE
101. I'LL MEET YOU BY THE RIVER
103. I'M GONNA KEEP ON
106. I'M SAVED AND I KNOW THAT I AM
107. I'M WINGING MY WAY BACK HOME
109. I'VE BEEN TO CALVARY
111. I'VE BEEN WITH JESUS
113. I'VE NEVER BEEN THIS HOMESICK BEFORE

115. I'VE NEVER SEEN THE RIGHTEOUS FORSAKEN
119. IF IT KEEPS GETTIN' BETTER
121. IN THE SHELTER OF HIS ARMS
122. IT IS FINISHED
124. IT WILL BE WORTH IT ALL
125. IT WON'T RAIN ALWAYS
128. IT'S BEGINNING TO RAIN
130. JOHN THE REVELATOR
132. LIFT ME UP ABOVE THE SHADOWS
136. LOOK ON THE BRIGHTER SIDE
139. LOOK WHAT THE LORD HAS DONE
143. LORD, FEED YOUR CHILDREN
145. LOVEST THOU ME
146. MIDNIGHT CRY
148. MIRACLES WILL HAPPEN ON THAT DAY
151. MORE OF YOU
153. NO ONE CARED SO MUCH
155. NO TEARS IN HEAVEN
156. NOTHING'S TOO BIG FOR MY GOD
159. NOW I HAVE EVERYTHING
160. O FOR A THOUSAND TONGUES
161. OH, HOW MUCH HE CARES FOR ME
163. ON THE SUNNY BANKS
165. OUT OF HIS GREAT LOVE
166. OVER THE MOON
168. SING YOUR BLUES AWAY
171. SPEAK TO THE MOUNTAIN
173. SUNDAY MEETIN' TIME
175. THANK GOD FOR THE PROMISE OF SPRING
176. THANK GOD I AM FREE
178. THAT OLD TIME PREACHER MAN
180. THAT'S ENOUGH
184. THE ALTAR
187. THE HAVEN OF REST
188. THE LORD STILL LIVES IN THIS OLD HOUSE
190. THE LOVE OF JESUS
192. THE NIGHT BEFORE EASTER
194. THE NINETY AND NINE
195. THE OLD FASHIONED MEETING
197. THE PRETTIEST FLOWERS WILL BE BLOOMING
200. THE STATUE OF LIBERTY
202. THE WICKED SHALL CEASE THEIR TROUBLING
205. THE WORLD DIDN'T GIVE IT TO ME
208. THERE IS A RIVER
210. THIS GREAT CARAVAN KEEPS ON ROLLING ALONG
212. TO ME, IT'S SO WONDERFUL TO KNOW JESUS IS MINE
214. TRUST AND OBEY
215. WAIT'LL YOU SEE MY BRAND NEW HOME
218. WHAT A LOVELY NAME
221. WHEN HE BLESSED MY SOUL
223. WHEN I GOT SAVED
225. WHEN JESUS SAYS IT'S ENOUGH
228. WHEN THEY RING THE BELLS OF HEAVEN
230. YES, I KNOW!
231. YOU AND ME JESUS

SOUVENIR SONGBOOK SOUVENIR SONGBOOK
SOUVENIR SONGBOOK
SOUVENIR SONGBOOK
SOUVENIR SONGBOOK
SOUVENIR SONGBOOK
SOUVENIR SONGBOOK